HALLARD PRESS

2368 Branchville Terrace
The Villages, FL 32162
352-234-6099
HallardPress.com
Info@HallardPress.com

Hallard Press LLC is a private, independent (indie) publishing house providing customized book and story editing, design, and publishing services for independent authors.

The Later Adventures of Don Quixote

A Memoir

by
Richard A Wanner
with
John W Prince

Edited by
Rebecca Henderson

**Book Design & Production
Hallard Press LLC**

THE LATER ADVENTURES OF DON QUIXOTE: A MEMOIR
OF RICHARD A WANNER
Copyright © 2023 RICHARD A WANNER
All rights reserved.

Cover Design, Typography, & Production
by Hallard Press LLC
Cover Images: Adobe Stock

Published by Hallard Press LLC.
www.HallardPress.com
Info@HallardPress.com 352-234-6099

Publisher's Cataloging-in-Publication data

Names: Wanner, Richard A., 1934-, author. | Prince, John W., author.
Title: The later adventures of Don Quixote : a memoir of Richard A. Wanner / Richard A. Wanner; with John W. Prince.
Description: The Villages, FL: Hallard Press, 2023.
Identifiers: LCCN: 2023909987 | ISBN: 978-1-951188-89-4 (hardcover) | 978-1-951188-90-0 (paperback)
Subjects: LCSH Wanner, Richard A., 1934-. | Wanner, Richard A., 1934- --Family. | Pennsylvania--Biography. | Socialism--United States. | Taxation--United States. | BISAC BIOGRAPHY & AUTOBIOGRAPHY / Personal Memoirs | BIOGRAPHY & AUTOBIOGRAPHY / Political
Classification: LCC HB119 .W36 2023 | DDC 362.092--dc23

Printed in the United States of America

ISBN: (Paperback) 978-1-951188-89-4

ISBN: (Hardcover) 978-1-951188-90-0

ISBN (ebook) 978-1-951188-91-7

"I know that if heaven exists and it represents perfection, then in some way Marie will find a hidden side entrance for me."

—Dick Wanner

Marie and I dance at our wedding.

Dedication

For Steve, Mike, and Jim, their families and children,
grandchildren and greats.
For all of our extended family.
Most of all for Marie. The love of my life.
—Dick

The Wanner grandchildren.
Top row L – R: Kate, Sarah, Zach. Bottom L – R: Jacob, Megan, Mitch.

Some writers look at a memoir as a chronicle of events happening in a chronological order. My own view of a memoir is events, remembrances, and emotions happening without too much regard for the calendar, interspersed with comments and other points of view, people, and events. Understanding this will prepare the reader of my memoir for the frequent change in both event timing and subject content. I wish you good luck as you progress through the memoir.

—Dick Wanner

To My Grandchildren

One important reason for writing this memoir is to communicate my ideas to my six grandchildren regarding what economic and cultural factors should be in place within the United States.

I do not expect them to adapt these concepts and ideas to themselves but only to understand what my thoughts are so they have a better understanding of their grandfather.

All six of them are adults, intelligent and successful, so it would be unreasonable for me to expect them to suddenly alter their established thoughts regarding the basic economic and cultural direction of our country.

I also want them to realize that I firmly believe my suggestions as presented within this memoir are necessary to prevent a socialist dominated government within the United States of America.

Miguel de Cervantes Saavedra *was an Early Modern Spanish writer widely regarded as the greatest writer in the Spanish language and one of the world's pre-eminent novelists. He is best known for his novel* Don Quixote, *a work often cited as both the first modern novel and "the first great novel of world literature."*

—Wikipedia

He served honorably under the Spanish flag at the Battle of Lepanto on October 7, 1571.

Born: 1547, Alcala de Henares, Spain

Died: April 22, 1616, Madrid, Spain

Children: Isabel de Saavedra

Spouse: Catalina de Salazar y Palacios (m. 1584–1616)

Nationality: Spanish

—Wikipedia

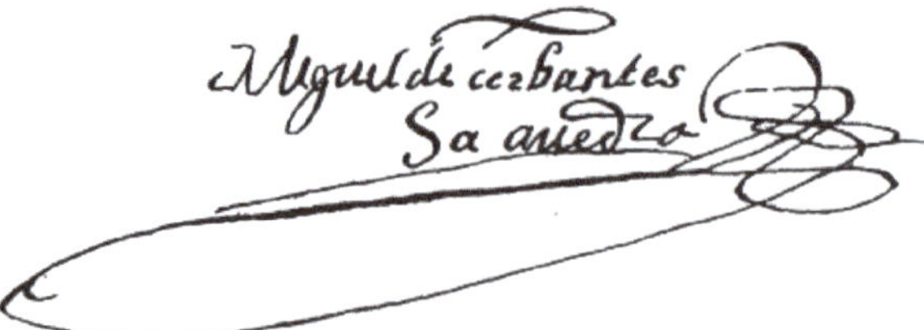

340.   Miguel Cervantes de Saavedra.

TABLE OF CONTENTS

Richard A. Wanner

Marie and me on our 60th Anniversary on one of our many anniversary cruises. This cruise, with the family, was to Alaska.

INTRODUCTION

BY JOHN W PRINCE

In case anyone asks, I'm a ghostwriter.

People, organizations, and companies come to me when they want words and content for a specific purpose. Some want to sell something or have others join them—so I write hundreds/thousands of words, combine the words and graphics, package them together in books, ads, articles, and media that get distributed to specific audiences.

I've written about/sold everything from copy machines to cheese to employee benefits.

Some people want a book about their life.

Now one commonality about what I do is that I seldom get credit for my contribution. However, Dick did include several positive references to my involvement and the impact they had on the overall content. I'm of the same generation as Dick Wanner, so many of his references are familiar to me. For that I thank him.

Many months ago, Dick Wanner asked me to help him with a project—to ghostwrite his memoir. I think he called it a "memoir" from the beginning. I called it a "personal history."

So began a long series of recorded interviews in his living room which were transcribed and became the basis for the "memoir." Dick began by telling me (several times) that he wanted his memoir to center on three areas:

1. To tell my story. To let people (my family, my descendants, my friends) know that I was here and what things were like during my time. Maybe to help explain why I am the way I am—or was. Which may help them explain why they are. Everyone is the sum of their past experiences and, certainly, some of my life has rubbed off onto others.

2. To tell Marie's story. We were together for 67 years. A decade longer than that if you count the years between kindergarten and high school. We're still together, actually. She started saving my life when I was 16, and kept saving it for nearly seven decades. Her story deserves to be told and remembered.

3. To tell a part of the story of America and offer a strategy for the future. For four intense years I was deeply indoctrinated into socialism by my father. I learned the structure and strategies of Socialism, Communism, and Fascism, how they originated and how they differed. With this information

Marie and her bridesmaids L-R: Ruth Stief (Marie's sister), Bobbi Egner, Marie, Lew Walters (Dick's sister).

Dick and his groomsmen L-R: Doug Walters (Lew's husband), Mike Shoppell (Dick's cousin), Dick, Jim Foreman (Marie's brother who gave her away), Jack Teasdale (Dick's cousin and best man).

"Marie and I were like Don Quixote and Sancho Panza in the Cervantes novel. As our sons said, "Dad made the plan and Mom made the plan work."

Sometimes my plans were not workable, but no matter, I had other backup plans that I could bring out at a moment's notice. We'd switch gears and plans and be off on another tack immediately."

No matter how crazy the plan, Marie always supported me."

(which is widely available, but seldom examined these days) I can see how and why our country is increasing the drift deeper into socialism. The drift, in my opinion, is reversible, but certainly not simple or easy.

Now all of this would be a heavy load even without trying to shoehorn in the taxation item. Dick could not predict, with any certainty, that his proposed National Acquisition Tax (NAT), was even remotely possible given the political state of the US and the world, and the fury of negative headwinds that such a proposal will generate. Plus, the concept had already been tried in various forms, without garnering sufficient support from the vast majority of the voting public.

"Dick is crazy," I soon decided.

Of course, there have been plenty of crazy people in the world, fictional and in real life. (IRL). My job was to find and compare the lives of Dick Wanner with some mythical person who makes their true calling the promotion of lost causes.

Known lost causes. Causes so lost that even the most ardent contender would not consider them.

Yes, I chose to compare Dick Wanner with that 17th century fictional hero and all round crazy Spaniard, Don Quixote. The Man of La Mancha. The Tilter of Windmills.

As Dick said in several ways during our interviews, "If someone told me it couldn't be done, I immediately went out and did it." Now if that doesn't sound like the old knight himself.

Dick would also tell everyone that he could not write. Not true. Dick was a very good writer. His problem is that he cannot spell and his handwriting or typing is quite slow and atrocious. But during his working life he often kept two typists busy transcribing his output. Dick wrote action-cause-consequence. If you do this then that will happen and the ultimate result will be such and such.

Emotion was not in his lexicon. Or, as we might say, emotion just did not compute.

That's why he had continuing emotional difficulties with his family. Oddly, Marie apparently seldom complained. The three boys, when asked in interviews for this memoir, said they never felt ignored or left out while growing up. One alluded to the premise that "Dad made the plan and Mom made the plan work."

So, Dick ended up writing much of the content for the National Acquisition Tax material in this book, leaving me with the emotional parts.

Some parts of the memoir were subject to discussion: abortion, how the tax would work, healthcare, and immigration were on the list. Of course,

Dick won most of those. "It's my book," he reminded me with a wry smile.

Marie died in 2020 of Progressive Supranuclear Palsy (PSP), a relatively rare and not-well-understood illness that mimics Alzheimer's and Parkinson's diseases. Google PSP and you'll learn more than you probably wanted to know. One of Dick's missions has been to spread awareness of PSP among both the medical and lay communities.

Dick's memoir is also very much a team effort.

During late 2022 and early 2023 I had some medical issues that prevented me from working on the content and design. Thanks to my business partner Nancy Hellekson for her hard work in keeping the project moving forward, and Rebecca Henderson for her sage editing and questioning that resulted in a much better book. And certainly thanks to Dick for his patience and loyalty.

Lest you think that Dick Wanner is less than superhuman, how about this:

In spring of 2023, at the tender age of 89, Dick participated in The Villages Senior Games and ran away with gold: 50 meters, 100 meters, and 200 meters in his age category 90-94. He was, or would be 90, during the year he competed.

Old Don Quixote would be impressed.

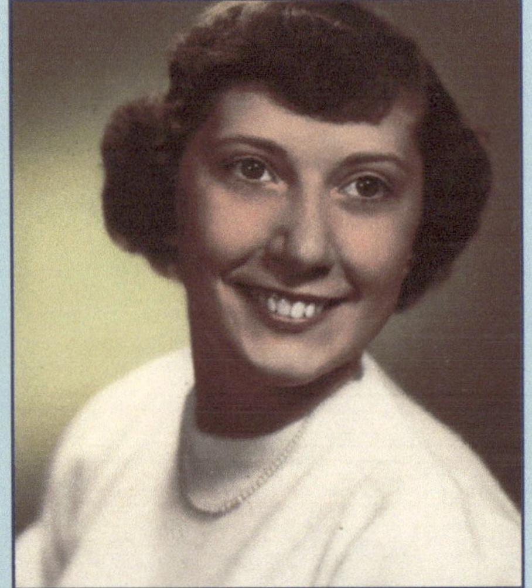

Graduation photos: Marie and Dick.

Marie as lead drum majorette. She led the group at a Macy's Thanksgiving Day Parade in New York City.

PLAYING THE ROLE OF SQUIRE SANCHO PANZA:

MARIE WANNER

While my approach to life has been somewhat "Quixotic," (Damn those windmills!) for some 67 years I had my own personal Sancho Panza close by my side. In Don Quixote, the book by Miguel Cervantes, squire Panza is portrayed as a rough and often-bumbling everyman who solves problems without the benefit of education or experience, an overweight and shambling man who has little time for appearances. But he is loyal to a fault, hoping for but seldom receiving a deserved reward, and ready to follow his master anywhere, even against his better judgment.

Marie was my Sancho, embodying only the best qualities—loyal, wise, all-seeing, and willing to put up with just about anything so long as we were in the same orbit.

Why did she choose me as her date for the Y-Teen Formal all of those years ago? The reason I want to believe is that maybe, for some quirky reason, she liked me.

Marie had many names: Gum, Mom, Mim—depending on who was speaking and the time of her life.

Marie grew up with many problems, not the least of which was initiating a relationship with me which was vehemently opposed by her friends, family, school, and (it seemed at the time) just about everyone else in the world.

My own mother, perhaps, was one of the few who approved.

Then there was the car accident while returning from a day visit during my Navy boot camp training. While she eventually "recovered," the issues from it continued to plague her for life.

There was an incredible amount of hard work while I pursued my ambitions, going to college while we all practically worked ourselves to death selling dogs and sodas on the Atlantic City Boardwalk. Three boisterous sons, my job changes, moves, and the normal curve balls that life sends your way.

Marie never complained (if she did, I don't remember it) and always went along with whatever I wanted.

Meanwhile, I hosted my own dark side.

*Marie and Dick. Ninth Wedding
Anniversary, 1962.*

*"Be a terror to the butchers,
that they may be fair in their
weight; and keep hucksters and
fraudulent dealers in awe, for the
same reason."*

—Cervantes

Too Young
Sung by Nat 'King' Cole

*They try to tell us we're too
    young*

Too young to really be in love

They say that love's a word

A word we've only heard

*But can't begin to know the
    meaning of*

*And yet we're not too young to
    know*

*This love will last though
    years may go*

*And then some day they may
    recall*

We were not too young at all

*And yet we're not too young to
    know*

*This love will last though
    years may go*

*And then some day they may
    recall*

We were not too young at all

Source: Musixmatch

Songwriters: S. Dee / S. Lippman

Too Young lyrics © Campbell Connelly And
Co. Ltd., Edward Proffitt Music, Aria Music
Co

For my first 16 years I was a chip in a maelstrom, never knowing what was going to happen next (bad or good), and living day to day, event to event. I developed an attitude.

Until Marie invited me to the formal dance, I was a kid without a conscience. If I inadvertently caused harm to a person there was no compassion or remorse to acknowledge my action. Please, thank you, I'm sorry were not words or terms that frequently passed through my lips. In business I could make an announcement that might negatively alter the lives of dozens of people without any outward concern for their position. If the change I created produced a profitable outcome for the company, then suck it up and move onto the next challenge was my normal attitude.

On the home front, it was my way or the highway.

I made decisions and Marie and the boys fell in line. I might be difficult to live with—moody, grumpy, sullen—that's the way things were. There were no apologies.

I felt that, because of all of the ordeals I had put up with, my conduct would be accepted, ignored, and even hidden.

Now let's get real.

The abuse that I administered to my family was not similar or equivalent to what I had been subjected to. But abuse can take numerous forms, and some are probably more painful than physical. I employed the more subtle mental forms.

Marie had a boundless supply of love for everyone and showed it always. Me, I was full of demons—or so I thought at times.

As I write this Marie has been gone for two-plus years. I've had some time to reflect, talk with my family, think about these things as I lay back on my lanai listening to my favorite birds. Learning for some is quick and painless. In my case it has been long, and with a great sense of remorse for my attitude during most of the ups and downs of life. Always looking inside myself and attempting to see a path to the future.

The answer is so simple and obvious. My villains, who treated me badly, were past victims themselves, paying their hate forward just as I was doing, thinking it would make a difference. I realized that my attitude was seriously flawed and would have no effect on those that abused my sister Lew and me. After all, they died years ago and the attention I gave them was a waste of my precious time. I regret that Marie is no longer here to share my conversion and participate in the joy that comes from living without my demons.

After Marie passed I wrote a long and rambling eulogy blaming myself (among other factors) for the discomfort that I caused her. I wanted to read it at a memorial service, but cooler heads prevailed, and it remained largely unread. Looking back, I believe it was my way of trying to deal with the grief and loss. I blamed the handiest person—me.

As so often happens, among all of the dreck and dross of my essay, one sentence stood out as a shining example of how I felt about Marie and what our life together was about:

"Also, I know that if Heaven exists, and that it represents perfection, then in some way Marie will find a hidden side entrance for me." (I actually wanted the last phrase to be the title of my memoir - John suggested a reference to Don Quixote would be a better title). What do you the reader Think?

Marie and I had our roles. We never laid them out in a formal script; they just sort of happened organically.

I was the "Don Quixote" with the windmills in the offing. "I want to go to college," kind of statement. And off I'd ride. I had a plan. And if that didn't work out, well I had another plan. If graduating from college was not the magic potion, was not as great as I thought it would be, oh well, I had other plans.

Marie was my faithful Sancho Panza. Maybe she believed that this was her role and she embraced it happily. As the boys have said, "Dad made the plan and Mom made sure the plan worked."

She was able to tolerate my brain that never stopped generating new ideas. She was stolidly supportive when I took on additional projects at work (without giving up the ones I already had). Marie just smiled and fell into step.

LIFE IS A SERIES OF STEPS

The human mind/body is a marvelous thing. It can take all kinds of punishment and injury, clamber back, and go on to do incredible things.

Marie was severely injured in the auto accident in 1951, And, at first, was not expected to live. Then she got past that and, while expected to live, was told she would never walk again and certainly would not be able to have children. Then, next diagnosis, was informed that she would no doubt walk again and would be able to have children.

From zero to a hundred miles an hour in a few months.

Life was not without stumbles over the years, but we managed it. I tilted at the windmills and Marie remained my loyal and wise companion. The boys grew, became men, married, and had their own families.

In May 1989 I retired from New Holland after 22+ years of dedicated service. We had been bought out by Ford, a logical buy for everyone concerned, except me because I would not mesh well

Dick Wanner recounts the details of his wedding day.

"My buddies and I celebrated far too much the night before and were wasted. As the ceremony time, 4:30 p.m., approached, Aunt Laura Teasdale got me out of bed, washed, shaved, dressed me in my wedding suit and, somehow, took me to the side entrance of the church just as Marie started up the aisle.

"She never panicked—even though other members of the bridal party did—because she knew that I would be there.

"Thank you, Aunt Laura. you saved the day."

The Cycle of Abuse

In 1979 American psychologist Lenore E. Walker created the phrase, "Cycle of Abuse," in which she explains patterns of behavior in an abusive relationship. Abusive and dysfunctional relationships tend to get passed down through the generations.

I agree with her.

My childhood traumas inured me from any remorse. That carried over into my adult life and my relationship with Marie and the boys.

with the Ford policies and culture. My solutions were targeted and "one-off" for the company—Ford was "by the book."

Marie and I moved to Salem, SC where Jim and I tried several business models over the next eight years until we found one that had legs. Steve and Mike did not accompany us and continued with their wives and families getting along in life, primarily based on their own skills and motivation.

During that time Marie was our "company office," secretary, mentor, wife, mother, and all-round Sancho Panza to the business as well as wife, mother, grandmother, wise counsel, and "Gum" to the whole extended family. She never complained; she just got things done.

Having found a Document Management System that had the required traction and that Jim could manage, Marie and I moved to The Villages, FL in 1997, looking forward to many fun years together enjoying the amenities of the world's biggest 55+ community.

Of course, that's when things started to fall apart.

She was diagnosed with pancreatitis a year later and spent five weeks in an ICU unit in nearby Ocala hospital.

Pancreatitis is a swelling and inflammation of the pancreas, a very serious and sometimes fatal condition.

It's often caused by heavy use of alcohol or gallstones and the condition cannot be cured, only managed through lifestyle changes and medication. Her doctors insisted that Marie had to be an alcoholic. Another incorrect diagnosis by a medical professional.

I transferred Marie to the University of Florida Shands Hospital in Gainesville, and within a day she was diagnosed with a blockage in a duct that descended from her gallbladder into her duodenum. Weeks of rest were needed to restore her health, so surgery could be performed.

All was good for about 10 years. She won a 5K road race, we traveled extensively, played golf, and using hindsight, waited for the next shoe to drop. A major back issue, operation, and a stroke while she was on the operating table, forced another move and the hope that she could move forward in life.

Then I collapsed and spent four days in hospital. We could no longer keep up and moved to Greenville, SC, close to family, and a small home in a continuing care facility. Marie did not improve. When people would ask about her my standard response was, "Same as yesterday."

Any change was always negative and depressing. It all seemed hopeless and there was little or nothing any of us could do. Marie also seemed to be suffering from the onset of dementia or Alzheimer's disease.

At Jim's suggestion Marie entered a federal program for stroke victims at the Medical University of South Carolina and underwent considerable testing to determine if improvement was possible regarding the stroke. One of her consultants suggested that Marie did have a stroke but that was not her primary problem. He suggested we visit with a neurologist for additional analysis. We did as recommended and the eventual finding was Progressive Supranuclear Palsy (PSP). I reported on PSP previously, but some additional information might be helpful.

Describing the woman you have deeply loved for decades, the mother of your children, in a few unemotional medical phrases does not do justice to the person. I take it personally and want to scream and hit something. "No! You're wrong." So, I believe, do our sons and their families and our grandchildren.

"It gets worse over time. There is no cure." Those are the only words you really hear. "Manage the symptoms."

The doctors were right. It got worse. Marie died on September 17, 2020, a few days after accusing me of leaving her in the night after promising to stay by her side. She was too ill to speak or touch me after that. I also took it personally. I had failed her at the last minute, thinking of my own comfort and not hers.

It's like a stubborn stain on a prized rug. No matter how many times you clean it, it will never completely go away. And, as a reminder, you see it again and again every time you cross the floor.

Most PSP patients live for five or six years. Marie lived for eight. A loyal and faithful Sancho Panza.

AFTER MARIE I RESET MY TRIM AND CARRIED ON.

I moved back to The Villages in Florida into the fourth home I have owned in this adult-centered paradise. Without Marie I carry on, too.

I exercise, golf, travel, and I'm very social (my Thirsty Thursday friends will vouch for that).

During the recent The Village Senior Games I actually won three gold medals, the 50, 100, and 200 meter dash events for men in the 90 to 94 age group. Most of the current friend base is 12 to 15 or more years younger than me but my age does not seem to matter.

I thank my lucky stars that I picked my current home in this small section within The Villages. Neighbors abound and they strive to keep me young and active. I love them all, each and every one.

My brain never rests. I have my passions and causes. Just ask me. I dare you!

Second grade class photo. Marie Foreman (happy and smiling) is 5th from the left in the second row from the back and I (morose and gloomy) am 5th from the left in the second row from the front. The guy in the front right either is trying to escape without anyone noticing, or has to go to the bath-room.

A RANT IN TIME

"The income tax has made more liars out of the American people than golf has. Even when you make a tax form out on the level, you do not know when it is through, if you are a crook or a martyr."
—Will Rogers

As any decent writer will tell you, writing a book gives you a soapbox to stand on and a megaphone to shout through. There's a certain level of effort expended, trees sacrificed, and distribution channels enabled, which most people agree gives you some credibility and standing. Sometimes the result is called a "rant."

There is also a grave danger that your audience will walk away because they disagree with your position, don't have the time or interest to listen any longer, or their phone buzzes with a text to pick up their child at daycare. Sometimes this is called a "distraction."

This is probably my rant. I've tried to make it as entertaining as possible, informative, personal, and relevant.

Anyway, it's fundamental to things we'll talk about later.

These first of the following three Amendments to the US Constitution allowed legalized theft by the government of the United States. The last two related to the prohibition on the sale of alcohol. The story of these amendments will occupy a large amount of space within my memoir.

•The 16th Amendment to the US Constitution, which gave Congress the power to levy and collect taxes on income, was ratified on February 3, 1913.

•The 18th Amendment was ratified on January 16, 1919, prohibiting the manufacture and sale of beverage alcohol (liquor).

•The 21st Amendment, repealing Prohibition, (and also the 18th Amendment) was ratified on December 5, 1933.

By that time the damage had been done. All of the sources of funding for the US government (and a long list of other items) had been completely changed in 14 years.

A few comments:

There is a direct relationship among these amendments that fundamentally changed the culture, laws, political views, and direction of the United States.

With the introduction of a progressive tax on income, the United States no longer had to rely on the liquor excise

Tributes in postage stamps.

Nations often pay tribute to historical events, famous people and the arts through their postage stamps. The Union of Soviet Socialist Republics (USSR) honored him with this stamp.

Marx and Lenin, authors of the 10 Planks of the Communist

Manifesto, also got their share of accolades on a Soviet stamp.

In addition to the tributes and education, nations also derived additional revenue from the sale of new issues to international stamp collectors.

tax along with the import tariffs to fund the country. This had a direct impact on national and international growth (the government had more money) and allowed the 18th Amendment that outlawed the manufacture and sale of liquor.

Although there were less than 14 years between the ratification of the 18th and 21st Amendments (which repealed the 18th) that short time span allowed for:

The growth spurt of organized crime fueled by activities such as unlawful gambling, loan sharking, prostitution, the sale of illegal drugs and alcohol, and other actions. We are still dealing with the devastating fall out almost a century later.

The growth spurt of socialistic thinking in the US fueled by the increased need for centralized law enforcement, international relations, the military, and communications.

As my father often noted, the passage of the income tax embodied in the 16th Amendment was one of the most significant events in American history. While many people would agree for various reasons, Al Wanner saw everything through the lens of socialism. It was, for him, the open door that allowed socialism to march on in the country. Even though most "socialists" in the country rebranded to become

"Democrats" in the 1940s, they did not abandon their aim of establishing socialism as the ruling (and perhaps only) political party.

It was, as Marx would state proudly, the second plank of the Communist Manifesto: A Heavy Progressive or Graduated Income Tax.

Whether the fulfillment of this plank in America was the result of good management, or good luck, (or a combination of both) is a matter of debate. Socialism took their wins where they could find them and celebrated.

One might argue that if Russian Minister of War Alexander Kerensky had not continued Russia's participation in the First World War, the Bolshevik Revolution would not have taken place and Vladimir Lenin would not have become the head of the government of Soviet Russia for seven years. Although Kerensky was a socialist, Lenin was a Marxist-socialist, and a leader of the October Revolution who was not afraid to massacre or incarcerate tens of thousands of people who did not agree with him. That allowed Josef Stalin, who followed Lenin as leader, to make the Communist Party into the vehicle for a totalitarian dictatorship that ordered political repression and mass murders. Socialism at its finest!

Of course, there are plenty of other "what ifs" that could be cited as flukes of history that allowed socialism to grow, and exhibit brief flashes of power in the United States. Including cities like Reading, which, when I was growing up, was led, and run by unabashed socialists. Including my father.

Whether my mother was a "true" socialist, or whether she just followed my father's lead, I'm not sure.

The only socialist direction she gave was ordering me to join a church (which may have been an order from my father), and then vetoing my first choice.

Obviously, she knew the requirement (I needed to be seen as an "upstanding Protestant Christian" in the community as part of my credibility if I was to be a future socialist leader).

My father died when I was sixteen—outside of infancy, I only lived and interacted with him for four-and-a-half years—but those few teenage years had a profound impact on my life. My mother passed away when she was 82 (and I was 49) and I don't remember her as other than a loving grandmother to our sons; and an intermittently loving, and sometimes hostile, mother.

She was instrumental in the breakthrough that brought me into the reading world. She was able to pinpoint the basic problem and propose a solution, even though trained educators either did not know, or did not care. To

me, that showed that she did actually care, although I don't remember her ever showing any real affection to either my sister Lew or me. We certainly were not a "hugs and kisses" family. Maybe Mom did not know how to express love to her children because of her own difficult childhood.

POLITICS MAKES STRANGE BEDFELLOWS

Though one might argue that the Temperance movement in the US was not "political," it certainly was in my estimation. Dating back to the early 1800s, many Americans believed that drinking liquor was immoral, destructive to individuals and families, and an existential threat to the very fabric of the country. They came together in a loose-knit coalition of groups and organizations, often spearheaded by church leaders, mostly women, and employing various. strategies to rid the nation of "the demon rum."

By the 1840s the American Temperance Society, headquartered in Boston, boasted over 8,000 chapters and more than one million members (in a country of only 17 million) who took a pledge to abstain from drinking distilled beverage alcohol.

Interestingly, beer and wine were not included among the proscribed drinks. In many early US urban areas, beer, wine, and distilled beverages were the only uncontaminated drinks available.

Potable water was simply unavailable, and water-borne diseases were common.

In the early 1870s another group started to coalesce under the banner of the Women's Christian Temperance Union(WCTU) led by Frances Willard.

As time went on, they moved on from promoting abstinence to the outright prohibition of alcohol.

The Temperance movement had a point. The drink had destroyed countless lives and families. I will relate in future sections of the memoir how booze has helped destroy people in my own family. It was the same or worse with many others.

However, the passage of the 16th Amendment made a fundamental change in the way that America was funded. The country was no longer heavily dependent on liquor taxes. Eliminating them would no longer endanger the finances of the country.

Add to that the weight of the socialists, who saw Prohibition as another opportunistic lever in their goal of establishing a socialistic culture, and the result was inevitable.

In 2014 Cato Institute published Bootleggers and Baptists: A Winning Combination by Adam Smith and Bruce Yandle (Executive Director of the Federal Trade Commission in the 1980s) about how unlike organizations can come together to accomplish social and other goals and, often, the very different motivations they had for the marriage of convenience.

The motivation behind the temperance organizations was clear-cut and obvious. The socialists were rather more devious.

Their policy was, I believe, to bring the United States down to the common level of the prevailing socialist countries.

THE NATIONAL TEMPERANCE ALPHABET

TWENTY-SIX PEN PICTURE STUDIES

OF

THE DRINK PROBLEM

BY

THOMAS R. THOMPSON

Published for General Distribution. Issued also in booklet form as Drinklets, Size 5 x 7 and also as a Folding Drop Post Card

PRICES ON APPLICATION

ADDRESS

THOS. R. THOMPSON, NEW HAVEN, CONN.

My father, referencing others, continually said the US was "too rich, too powerful, too many other things." They felt that their role was to reduce the stature of the US and blunt the driving force it had in world affairs.

There are individuals and organizations in the country, decades later, dedicated to this objective.

My way of thinking is that we should be trying to enhance our stature so that other countries see the US and try to emulate our success in a non-military way. In many ways, we have achieved that goal—however fleetingly. We have fences and security to keep people out— not to keep our own citizens in—unlike many socialist/Communist nations.

I embrace the notion of the "shining star on the hill" as Confucius. noted, "governments should serve the people," not the other way around. Otherwise, democracy as I understand it today, could be replaced by a more fanatical form of socialism.

In my analysis, based on my reading and the many conversations with my father, the socialist movement joined the temperance groups because they could see both a strong social and monetary incentive. Socially, Prohibition was a form of mass control over the entire population—helping to fulfill various aspects of Karl Marx's 10 Planks.

Socialists, I believe, also saw the potential for massive financial gain, and power, by controlling the import, manufacture, and sale of liquor.

As a microcosm of America, Reading was a city where drinking was a way of life for many—women as well as men.

It helped blunt the constant pain. There was deep corruption within the city and the administration. The "Jewish Mafia" allegedly led by the Minker brothers, Abe and Alex, controlled prostitution, gambling, drugs, and other illicit, but popular, activities. They also owned and operated legitimate businesses that helped launder the illegal money. Now, if alcohol were to be prohibited, the profits from illegal distribution and sale could be astronomical.

While the socialists and temperance people decided to jump into bed together to bring about change, I do believe that the socialists were happy with the arrangement, and ultimately, the temperance people were terribly disappointed.

The socialists had control and the criminals had money. Those with a foot in both of those camps scored the daily double. Temperance advocates lost big time. Not only was drinking not abolished, but it also probably increased as the lure and glamor of the speakeasy lifestyle enveloped the

Continued from previous page.

7. Extension of factories and instruments of production owned by the state; the bringing into cultivation of waste.

8. Equal obligation of all to work. Establishment of Industrial armies, especially for agriculture.

9. Combination of agriculture with manufacturing industries; gradual abolition of the distinction between town and country by a more equable distribution of the population over the country

10. Free education for all children in government schools. Abolition of children's factory labor in its present form. Combination of education with industrial production.

country, embarrassing and angering the teetotalers.

By the end of Prohibition, only a few years later, the socialist cause had been enhanced as income tax and many of the sociopolitical controls remained in place. The Mafia lost a revenue source, but it had been a windfall for them anyway, and they had plenty of other income streams as illegal drugs became more popular.

The mainstream Prohibitionists fell out of favor, and we hear little from them anymore.

When I explain this to contemporary people they often nod wisely and change the subject. What I want them to say is, "What should we do? How could we change things?"

OK. Since you were kind enough to have asked, here goes:

One item that would make a difference: We (the United States) could start by not sending any more "hawks" or "useful idiots" as diplomats to other countries. Our diplomats should encourage all countries to adopt a more realistic approach to government that would emphasize the need for the government to serve the people. Of course, this is an idealistic approach; one that may be impossible to achieve. There will always be Hitlers, Stalins, Pol Pots, and Idi Amins that need to be put down.

Ambassadorships are usually a factor of how much money or endorsement the potential ambassador has contributed to the ruling party. A plum ambassadorship is to the UK—Ambassador to the Court of St. James—which was given to Joseph P. Kennedy (father of President John F. Kennedy and others), for a couple of years in the late '30s by President Franklin D. Roosevelt. Kennedy resigned the ambassadorship after two years, embroiled in a host of gaffes and controversies.

In the recent past, "The West" has acted as a bulwark restraining Soviet and (to some extent) Chinese expansion. But that temper seems to have diminished in US foreign policy. We withstood the long Cold War, the Korean Conflict, The Berlin Wall, Vietnam (a dubious venture), and other larger and smaller incursions to prevent the spread of "Communism."

To what avail? The current American strategy seems to be to apologize, bow, beg forgiveness, and self-flagellate forever.

We do not enter expensive wars to "win," but to satisfy some vague social goal that neither changes anything in the long run, nor satisfies anyone.

Russia (Putin) would never allow Ukraine to become a NATO member. So, even after fruitless diplomatic efforts, the only Russian strategy that worked was invasion. If you asked 1,000 American students to point out the Ukraine on a map, most would fail. The lack of education on vital subjects in American schools is at the root of America's downfall. How do you educate people on places they know nothing about and can't even find on a map?

Let's teach geography—a subject that is not taught after seventh grade these days. What about history? These subjects, along with math and English are far more important to America's future.

I am suggesting that the relationships we establish diplomatically should be organized to encourage countries to adopt an economy and culture that benefits its people. Guns and tanks should not be our first approach to international diplomacy. As an immigration issue for the United States, people, regardless of their country of origin, that are happy and content, will generally stay put. Not travel thousands of miles to obtain these desirable human objectives. Freedom and prosperity should be the norm, not the exception for all of mankind.

Then we have Americans who travel to foreign countries and never see or experience anything remotely foreign.

They fully expect bacon and eggs with Diet Coke for breakfast.

For example:

I was on a US tour from the Spanish city of Ceuta across the Straits of Gibraltar from European Spain. It took almost two hours to get through customs into Morocco. A problem began when the Moroccan customs officials came on board and said, "You must turn over your passports to us for inspection."

Now this procedure is not unusual.

If you are on an overnight train that crosses a European border, the conductor will normally collect passports before the passengers go to sleep and, after the inspection at the border, return them to the passengers when they awake in the morning. I have never heard of anyone losing their passport in the process.

On the trip to Morocco, about 20 percent of the travelers, virtually all American, kept their passports, got off the bus, and went back to Ceuta. I wanted to see something of Morocco, so I surrendered my passport and waited— over two hours, as it turned out—until we were all inspected and ready to go. But it gave us all an opportunity to get to know each other better.

We rolled along for a couple of hours when some of the passengers began to call for a bathroom stop. Our English-speaking guide spoke to the driver who eventually pulled over to the side of the road. There was a small shed and a thick hedge. "Women behind the hedges. Men behind the building," our guide announced. You'd think that he had just announced the end of the world was on the horizon.

To generalize, Americans, including our diplomats, tend to have little knowledge of the world and its people.

There are Americans who say, "Why should I travel to other countries? We've got everything we need here in the good, old US of A."

They may be beyond help.

A few men got off and ducked in behind the shed. The women never got off the bus. They gamely held on until we reached our destination and, some in obvious agony, hiked up an enormous hill to the hotel facilities.

For most Moroccans, dodging behind a hedge in the middle of nowhere to answer calls of nature was not unusual—of course they would prefer a nice bathroom, but the bush will do in an emergency. Too many Americans, intolerant and not knowledgeable, expect that the rest of the world to be just like their downtown hometown. When it is not, they hold their pee, sit in agony, and whine that this country is a terrible, primitive place.

At the hotel there was another cultural flash. The swimming pool was the center of activity with many guests clad in their bikinis and colorful trunks. On the other side of a rather high concrete wall, women were completely covered by their burqas. The hotel was a tourist trap—emulating an American resort in Florida—collecting American dollars, euros, and pounds so tourists could hang out in a foreign country in an environment that was just like home.

In total, most of the American tourists learned absolutely nothing about Morocco, the people, culture, food, manners, or anything else. But they could announce to their friends that in Morocco their hotel had a nice pool, but that the locals thought peeing behind a bush was OK.

In the early '60s President John F. Kennedy developed a unique concept that became known as the Peace Corps.

Young people loved it and thousands went overseas to interact directly with people in many countries. It was very successful for two reasons: Both sides learned a good deal from each other.

Americans learned the customs, culture, and civilization of the people they visited. They learned how diverse the world really is and that many practices we might find strange or offensive, are correct and dignified given the different circumstances. They learned that people are generally good, generous, and welcoming everywhere.

The hosts learned that not all Americans are ugly, loud, and aggressive. They also learned something of democracy, capitalism, and innovation.

Unfortunately, we export our military assets so that local governments can either (a) overthrow the current political system or (b) maintain the current political system. Sometimes a bit of both. We supported Chavez in Venezuela until he revealed that he was Communist, then we pivoted to support the opposition.

In most of our international meddling we are not looking at what the local people want, we are looking at what is best for the United States at the moment, reserving the right to quickly change our minds at will.

There is intolerance worldwide. No matter what country you might mention, certain groups are repressed, marginalized, and in some cases, eliminated. The Dalits in India, Rohingyas in Myanmar, Uyghurs in China—to mention only three. Usually, the repression is based on ethnicity or religion—or both.

Oddly, the authorities can overlook certain individuals or groups who display a particular talent of skill that is in high demand. Years ago, when General Nassar was ruling Egypt, he ordered the country's Coptic Christians (who make up about 10 percent of the population) into a desolate, hilly area outside Cairo where water was scarce, believing that they would die out or leave the country. If my memory serves me correctly the Hill was known in Cairo as Mokattam.

After the initial shock, they became the trash collectors for Cairo, picking out the valuable materials for recycling and sale. They chopped an amazing outdoor cathedral from the living rock of a mountainside, found water sources, and created a thriving city of their own.

When I visited, along with our hosts for the Egyptian vacation (Mel and Dona Ward) they welcomed us as Americans and noted that the US was a country to emulate in their struggle, even though they were a repressed minority in a Muslim country.

But the story is not over yet.

We also went to a performance of the Cairo Opera. We were in the second row and could see everything on stage in great detail. When the diva, the lead soprano, came on stage I noticed that she was wearing a small cross on her neck chain—which undoubtedly marked her as a Coptic Christian.

Although she was a member of a shunned religious group, her exceptional talent overcame the normal biased nature of the audience and leads me to have faith that there is room for acceptance in a world that is getting more tolerant of religious and cultural differences.

It is also sometimes puzzling to me that people in some countries that could be classified as "strongly socialist" will put their lives on the line and rebel against their totalitarian masters. Take Hungary in the 1950s, or Czechoslovakia which rebelled and gained a much-increased level of freedom. Rebels in Tunisia started the Arab Spring movement and, although they are now regressing back to a dictatorship, it appears the notion of freedom is still present. The Libyan liberation was certainly a military one, but it had the support of most of the population that desired a more freedom-based system.

The process of exporting "prosperity" would be a long one—a century or more before it stuck. Also, Americans are tired of warfare, particularly wars that are lost because we the people, are not prepared to pay the cost in either dollars or lives. Nor are our political leaders prepared to fight to "win." All of these issues should serve to teach the US that the heavy hand of the remote bureaucrats will cause the system to fail.

We sometimes believe that "Communism" is a failed system because of the fall of the Soviet Union. But as my father taught me, hard core Communism was doomed to failure because of its bureaucratic overload. Fascism ("Communism lite" in my parlance), is the form of Socialism that has the best chance for success and represents what he thought would be the eventual form of a future United States government. A horror for me and a success for Al Wanner and all "tax the rich" thinkers.

I am not alone in looking for solutions to the income tax challenge.

There have been several serious attempts at reforming the income tax by creating an alternate system that was reasonably fair, simple to manage and maintain, quick and easy for taxpayers to file, yet raising enough money to fund the country.

Of course, there have been other attempts at simplifying the income tax "process"—but not the income tax "concept."

Let's pretend that we are starting a new country from scratch, much like our Founding Fathers. They did a pretty good job considering the culture and technology of the times (a communication to and from England took several weeks of tossing around on the Atlantic Ocean), and that a good deal of their deliberations took place in taverns.

The Founding Fathers could not have imagined the debt that their new country would have to take on to fulfill the destiny they helped set for it. While Alexander Hamilton was brilliant in being a leader of creating the Constitution, he did forget a few parts.

On the plus side, he advocated that debt be available for the new country. He understood we could not grow without the opportunity for debt, just like most of us could not buy houses without a mortgage. The parts that he forgot included some control on debt— there's nothing in the Constitution that addresses debt and very little regarding deficit spending. I assume that he believed that future generations would be wise enough to manage their borrowing. Sadly, that has not been the case.

So, now we have the opportunity (at least in "pretend land") to fix this oversight. What should we do?

First, let's look at what we have.

The Constitution uses the language that existed at that time. The legal language of 1787 that is used in the Constitution makes sense if you view it through the lens of time. At that time, it was very logical, widely understood, and it was the language that was used in the courts. But it does not contain the same clarity to many citizens that are living in the 21st century.

It is like the King James Version of the Bible which was published in 1611. Then, a few centuries later, people said, "I don't understand what that means." So, we had new translations of the Bible which brought the language up to date. Perhaps what we need is a contemporary interpretation or translation of the US Constitution. A plain language version of the Constitution if you will.

There is some danger in this, much like the Bible is subject to the interpretation of the translators when it moves from Hebrew to Latin to Greek to Arabic and back to Latin again. Then the King James Version was translated into the English of the day. There are all kinds of room for new interpretations, new ideas, and the deletion of ideas. At least with a plain version of the US Constitution were simply translating, or interpreting, the US English language of 1787 to the US English language of 2023. And at least we can easily refer back to

the original if there are any questions.

This is certainly not an original idea and you can find an excellent example by Googling. It also needs to be understood that the US Constitution was written as a political document. Although it was aspirational in nature, it was also couched in reality and was the work of a number of people including Alexander Hamilton and James Madison. The Founders understood that the Constitution had to be signed by a certain number of people and ratified by a majority of the 13 states. At best it was a compromise (as are most political documents), and to a large extent they were making it up as they went along.

I can just see them. They're over at the Tavern—not sitting around a table atIndependence Hall as many would believe— and they're saying among themselves "We want this to pass." John Jay, Alexander Hamilton, and James Madison are probably pushing the reality of that.

Someone asks, "How many votes do we have now out of the 13 states?" They start counting on their fingers and the number of votes they have is nine. "So, let's say we require that nine of the 13 states are needed to ratify theConstitution. Good, now let's move on to the next item."

If the founders had decided that it had to be a unanimous vote requiring

The Law of Unintended Consequences

There were also unintended consequences that the people who framed the amendment would never have thought of. For example, the IRS knows everything about everybody. Who would have thought that data capture would be a major result of the 16th Amendment. Of course, the IRS will contend that your tax returns are private. But as virtually everyone knows from the news, that is simply not true.

The Transition & Compromise

The transition from the Articles of Confederation to the United States Constitution wasn't a seamless one, and fixing the problems of the Articles of Confederation required a series of lengthy debates both during and after the convention. But one thing was certain, something had to be changed. Fifty-five Delegates met at the Constitutional Convention of 1787 to determine how best to adjust the existing document.

The Weaknesses of the Articles of Confederation were:

Each state only had one vote in Congress, regardless of size.

Congress didn't have the power to tax, or to regulate foreign and interstate commerce

There was no executive branch to enforce any acts passed by Congress

There was no national court system

Amendments to the Articles of Confederation required a unanimous vote

Laws required a 9/13 majority to pass in Congress

Continued...

13 states to approve, I believe they knew that they would have the states warring against each other and it would have been like Prussia all over again. "If Delaware won't agree, we'll invade them!"

The Constitution was written, signed, and gave the US a starting point for the creation of the country, but like many creations, time has ravaged it, compromises have been made, the structure is getting rickety, and we need to make some fundamental changes that will bring the wheels back into alignment.

One of those fundamental changes is in how we fund the country.

We have an income tax code that is tens of thousands of pages long. No one person understands it completely. It has more loopholes than can be counted, employs tens of thousands of workers, is eminently unfair to virtually every constituency, and enforcement is sporadic and random. Every year more pages are added.

Where do we go from here?

To make progress we need to change the concept of an "income tax" to the concept of an "acquisition tax" where Americans pay on what they buy (or consume), rather than on how much money they make this year.

My solution, which I will argue going forward, is "The NAT"—The National Acquisition Tax—which would be fair to everyone, simple to implement and enforce, easy to understand, and flexible as the world changes. Americans would have the freedom to pay more or less, depending on their buying decisions, and the nation would have the funding it needs to continue serving its citizens.

Another famous Marie & Dick anniversary cruise
—sailing into the sunrise.

...Continued

a great deal of interstate conflict, something that delegates, tried their best to solve. However, under the Articles, when the Founding Fathers signed the Constitution in 1787, it needed ratification from nine states before it could go into effect. This was not easy.

There were two sides to the Great Debate: the Federalists and the Anti-Federalists. The Federalists wanted to ratify the Constitution, the Anti-Federalists did not. One of the major issues these two parties debated concerned the inclusion of the Bill of Rights.

Both Hamilton and Madison argued that the Constitution didn't need a Bill of Rights, that it would create a "parchment barrier" that limited the rights of the people, as opposed to protecting them. However, they eventually announced a willingness to take up the matter of the series of amendments which would become the Bill of Rights. Without this compromise, the Constitution may never have been ratified by the States.

—ConstitutionalFacts.com

A Unique Weapon

The musket/long rifle with a six-sided barrel hanging on the mantle in the photo on the next page was found in a closet after Marie's Auntie Fischer died.

On a Wanner family visit to Colonial Williamsburg in Virginia, the gunsmith was asked if he had ever seen a six-sided barrel on such a weapon.

"No," was his respone. "There's never been one made." He seemed quite sure of that.

On a later visit to Colonial Williamsburg the gunsmith was shown the rifle and was astounded, deeming it an historic piece.

The rifle was refurbished by the gunsmith's team (they decided to leave it as a conversion to a percussion cap rather than reverting to the original flintlock version) and warned the Wanners not to fire the piece.

It is believed that the weapon was made by a gunsmith's apprentice in Bucks County, PA between 1780-1790.

The Wanner Family: Standing: Mike, Jim, Dick; Seated: Marie; Kneeling: Steve.

SOCIALISM, THE US, AND MY FATHER

To the average person, the concept of socialism is attractive at first.

Socialism as a concept assumes that all people are noble and selfless. However, like many concepts, it does not work in the real world because not all people are noble and selfless. Many are, unfortunately, despicable and greedy. All too often, the latter end up in control.

That may be a bitter pill to swallow for those people who want to believe in "the universal goodness of humanity." Take your own personal circle of friends and family. Some are good, some are just OK (depending on the day), and some are real villains. It's the latter group that makes a mockery of socialism and leads the good into slavery.

In a real-world Socialist scenario, the concept breaks down and a small number of power-hungry people end up with all of the power. The rest end up with no power, no toilet paper, pharmaceuticals, food, baby formula, or freedom. Completely subjugated by the powerful, they often end up in misery and grinding poverty.

For current examples see Venezuela, Cuba, and North Korea—among others.

According to my father, who was my teacher in all things socialist, socialism comes in several flavors.

The USSR after the 1917 revolution was Communist and characterized by completely unrealistic centralized Five-Year Plans, wide-spread famines, massacres of citizens, secret police, and government-controlled everything. It eventually collapsed under its own weight. (As my father predicted.)

North Korea is probably the strictest Communist state today. Totally controlled by a very small group of family and acolyte elites, access to virtually everything is tightly regulated. Famine is common, poverty the norm, concentration camps abound, and abject misery is endemic. Meanwhile, the elite live in splendor and luxury. The military has top priority in every area including food and other scarce resources.

Although we call the China of today "Communist," my father would call it Fascist. "Fascism," he believed, was a somewhat workable combination of socialistic requirements that allowed some tightly controlled private businesses and personal wealth within a strict government centered framework.

He would credit Italy's World War II dictator, Benito Mussolini, with implementing the concept, understanding that a modicum of freedom allowed the beneficial innovations of private enterprise while preserving the power of the central government. The culture portrayed in the film Schindler's List showed how Fascism and private enterprise could be sustained in a closed system.

China today allows a certain amount of freedom as long as the outcomes remain consistent with ever-changing goals and policies of the central Chinese Communist Party. The current (2023) chaotic situation in Hong Kong is evidence of the retaliation that can result when citizens and enterprises do not keep up with, or choose to challenge, the current rules.

Contemporary Cuba and Venezuela might be described as dysfunctional communist societies. While certain Americans will point out that in Cuba education and medical care are dispensed by the government at "no cost," they overlook the reality that the wages of most individuals are well below any reasonable poverty line, information and the media are tightly controlled, individual freedom is non-existent, citizens are arrested for protesting government policies, and people keep risking their lives trying to escape. The latter is a damning indictment of the political and social situations.

There are other countries that my father might classify as "hybrid fascist/ socialist:" Myanmar, Vietnam, Kazakhstan, for example.

Other countries might be termed "mildly socialist/fascist:" the Scandinavian nations, for example. "Free" education, childcare, medical care, and cradle-to-grave welfare are all part of the package there, and so is the tax rate which can exceed 70 percent of personal income. A Big Mac costs about twice as much in Stockholm as it does in Boise. There is no "free lunch," even in the Swedish capital.

So, there are "degrees" of Socialism/ Communism/Fascism around the world; some waxing and some waning over time.

In my father's time there were certainly pockets of rabid socialism in the United States—Reading, PA being one of them. But there were also great swaths of the nation that outright rejected socialism and fully embraced capitalism.

Today, I believe my father would be delighted that the entire United States is Socialist leaning—quickly moving toward full Socialism, probably using the Fascist approach.

AN ESSAY ON SOCIALISM, THE UNITED STATES, CONSTITUTIONAL AMENDMENTS, MY FATHER, AND ME

THE CONCEPT, EVOLUTION AND DESTINY OF SOCIALISM (IMHO)

Socialism, as a concept, goes back thousands of years, probably to the beginnings of humanity. Hunter-gatherers living in caves practiced a "communalism" in terms of hunting, food production, raising children, and shelter that was beneficial to all or most of the members of the community.

The difference between cave dwellers and modern hippie communes boils down to one of technology and the development of political systems.

Cave dwellers were socialist in application for pure survival reasons—the survival of a group was much more likely than the survival of an individual alone. I doubt if they questioned, much less analyzed, their choice. They were too busy trying to survive. Their idea of high technology might have been a pointed stick.

Modern commune dwellers are socialist for aesthetic and philosophical reasons. They are escaping a society or societal conditions they view as regressive or repressive. Usually, they have studied philosophies that offer guidelines on how such a community might operate. Their high technology would be a cell phone and a fast, reliable internet connection.

The communities of the cave dwellers survived for a long time because the concept offered tangible benefits to the individual. Over time they developed leadership, routines, and rituals that strengthened the bonds among the individuals and promoted prosperity for the group. Some individuals might rebel, but then the choices included biting one's tongue and submitting, joining another group, or going solo. Choosing the latter could mean starving or ending up as lunch for a saber-tooth cat.

Modern communes offer the companionship of like-minded individuals, but few other tangible benefits. Continuation requires the individual to submit to the will of the collective, which can be difficult, humans being as they are. There are those humans who naturally like to be in charge, and firmly believe that they should receive more than their share for their leadership.

Leadership often tends to become greedy and makes decisions that allow individual theft of resources, to the

When I mention the Socialist "movement" in the US (I label it a "slide") some people ask, "So when will full socialism be achieved?" I don't know the answer, Also, there are many countries that are way ahead of us in the slide. Notably most of Europe and especially Canada to our north.

In my personal estimation, I think that Canada is about 25 years ahead of the US.

detriment of the group. Some become more equal than others. If an individual in a modern commune rebels, going back to the general population does not have high risks. They can move back with their parents or friends. Welfare programs will provide food, shelter, and clothing. The risks of being eaten by a wild animal are minimal. The downsides to leaving the commune are mostly philosophical.

Therefore, I conclude that socialism among cave dwellers persisted for millennia because it provided tangible, measurable benefits in the face of a very risky world. Corrupt leadership might need to be purged once in a while, but the concept was sound. Being kicked out of the cave could be as good as a death sentence. As civilization mitigated the individual risks, the concept faded away because the purpose and value had disappeared.

Modern communes are subject to failure, most sooner than later, because the benefits they offer to members are not tangible or measurable, and because they are exceedingly subject to corruption by certain members. I'm suggesting that modern communes are the socialistic micro equivalent of the modern big government macro organizations.

Modern socialism often devolves into a "command leadership," or "cult of personality," where corrupt leadership steals the resources and power for their own enrichment, and enforces a belief system that makes them appear as benevolent "gods."

Another human failing that dooms socialism is that the concept offers no incentive for excellence or achievement. Since everyone gets the same share, at least in theory, there is no reason why anyone should try harder to accomplish anything.

HARMONY, INDIANA

One case in point is the tiny village of Harmony, Indiana founded on April 27, 1825, by British industrialist Robert Owen.

"There is but one mode by which man can possess in perpetuity all the happiness which his nature is capable of enjoying," Owen wrote. "That is by the union and cooperation of all for the benefit of each." Owen addressed his remarks to Congress and anyone else who would listen. His plan eventually attracted hundreds of leading thinkers, artists, scientists, and workers to help them create, "a superior social, intellectual, and physical environment," wrote Dan O'Donnell in a 2020 article for the MacIver Institute.

"This would be a community of equals unlike any the country has seen before. Each of Harmony's 800 residents would contribute their unique talents and share in the bounty that they were sure to produce together."

"While Owen's words were confident and uplifting, they didn't work," O'Donnell continues, "Almost immediately, Owen recognized that his grand community was chaotic. Its residents lacked the motivation to work, while its government was unable to manage even the town's one general store... The community couldn't produce enough food to be self-sufficient, primarily because when the hardest working members realized that they would earn the same benefits as the laziest, they stopped working. Within a year the perfect model of utopian socialism had failed."

Ordinary humans within a civilization, it appears, require incentives to produce. The concept of socialism, that everyone is equal and should receive the same benefits, sounds good but will always fail. This is a concept that my father and other socialists seemed unwilling, or unable, to comprehend. Perhaps it is because their particular brand of socialism offered incentives (money and power come to mind) for leaders who encourage (a good beating perhaps?) the ordinary people to stay in line and be productive.

Writers over the years have written and published stories and books detailing their view of life in a Socialist state.

The fable of The Little Red Hen, first collected by Mary Mapes Dodge in 1874, teaches much the same lesson. The little red hen nurtured her garden, collected wheat, ground flour, and made bread while the others lazed about. She therefore had food when the winter arrived. The others, who had not prepared, faced starvation, but fully expected to partake of the little red hen's bounty.

George Orwell published Animal Farm in 1945. It's a "beast fable" where the animals of the farm decide to take control using Socialist principles. They are betrayed and a pig named Napoleon takes over control of the animal community to the detriment of the non-pig members. The situation had become worse than before.

Orwell published "1984" in the summer of 1949. This dystopian social science fiction novel described life under a Socialist controlled government and all of its citizens.

Fahrenheit 451 (the temperature at which paper combusts) by Ray Bradbury was published in 1953. It presents an American society where books have been personified and outlawed and "firemen" burn any that are found.

There were warnings, but most people did not pay attention.

FINANCING SOCIALISM

THE WHISKEY REBELLION - A SHORT HISTORY OF THE TAX ON ALCOHOL

Between 1791 and 1794, the new United States, along with the new President Washington, had to suffer through the troubles generated by the Whiskey Rebellion (or Whiskey Insurrection), where the government tried to partially finance the country through a tax on distilled spirits.

The whiskey producers along the then-frontier (Western Pennsylvania) rebelled. It was, they said, too regressive that they had to travel to Philadelphia (300 miles) to appear in a Federal Court, and that their taxation rate was higher than the larger distilleries in the east.

Many western distillers refused to pay, skirmishes developed, people died, property was destroyed, and President Washington himself (wearing his Revolutionary War uniform) led federal troops into the area. There was virtually no actual combat as the farmers gave up their position and went home. A few were arrested but later pardoned. The encounter demonstrated that our new national government had the ability and will to suppress violence and establish laws to provide needed revenue for the fledgling country.

Eventually the Feds eliminated the tax on alcohol and, until the Civil War, relied on tariffs to finance the new government. The "Rebellion" helped establish the Power of the People to make (and break) the new laws and run the country as they felt best.

THE COST OF RUNNING A COUNTRY

When America was founded in September 1776 the Founding Fathers got many things right, but how could they foresee the cost of running a country that was joining the industrial age, expanding across a continent, and growing as a world power?

Funding for the new nation was inadequate, woefully evident as the War of 1812 raged between Britain and the new country, and the Civil War erupted in the spring of 1861. These, and other consuming needs, drained the treasury and the U.S. was forced into borrowing from other countries, and from their own populace with bond issues, to meet their obligations. In the beginning, the tax on beverage alcohol and tariffs on imported goods were the mainstay of the federal treasury.

Grain is easy to grow; difficult to transport. The more remote the grainfields from commercial centers, the more costly it was to get it to market. One thing farmers knew for certain: There was always a market for booze. So, they started up their own processing plants—distilleries—and shipped the output to an ever-thirsty market. Even George Washington distilled whiskey at Mount Vernon.

Liquor, for the most part, was not price sensitive, always in high demand despite the vocal teetotalling crowd, and easy to produce and transport. It was, in the government's view, an ideal and constant source of tax revenue. For many years America ran on the excise taxes on booze.

This also spawned a host of opportunities and problems.

Drunks (mostly men) became ubiquitous, ranging from my vicious and brutal drunken paternal grandfather, to the happy and friendly drunken maternal grandfather. In addition to everything else, their families suffered as they spent all the money on drink—a major social problem.

Crime was rampant. Everything from producing and selling untaxed alcohol, to various shades of theft for money to buy liquor abounded—a major crime problem.

The opportunities depended on which side of the law you were on.

For the average working man, a well-deserved drink or ten at the end of a long, hard day was part of the American Dream in the 1800s.

Booze and tariffs raised a ton of money, but it was never quite enough. I've heard estimates that back then as much as 70% of the country's revenue came from liquor taxes.

Alcohol was both a killer and a life saver.

During the Civil War, the U.S. flirted with an income tax which was levied and temporarily tolerated. Citizens earning over $600 a year paid 3% of their income; those making over $10,000 paid 5%. However, as soon as the war was over the tax was allowed to expire in 1872 and funding for the country returned to excise taxes and tariffs on imported goods.

The enterprising folks in Washington started looking for other sources of revenue. The one that seemed the most lucrative was an income tax. By the late 1800s America had an elementary banking system, a cohesive currency structure, and an economy that could be tracked. Although the barter economy was still strong, more and more workers were being paid in money, and ordinary consumer financial transactions were more likely to be done using cash.

In 1913, the 16th Amendment to the Constitution of the United States, introduced into Congress in 1909, was ratified by three-quarters of the states,

allowing Congress to levy and collect tax on income.

Pandora's box was flung open. Relatively simple in the beginning, it rapidly grew into the many-headed monster it is today. Generally supported by the states in the South and the West; Alabama was the first to sign.

The first tax schedule had seven brackets, ranging from 1% on the first $20,000 of income, to 6% on income exceeding $500,000. The intake for the first year of income tax amounted to $28.3 million (over $792 million in 2021 dollars).

Three items to note from my viewpoint:

1. The second Plank of Karl Marx's Communist Party Manifesto of 1848 (A Heavy Progressive or Graduated Income Tax) had been realized in this country.

2. My father taught me that the 16th Amendment was the key that unlocked the door to the advent of socialism in the United States.

3. From a broader perspective, the introduction of an income tax changed the essential character of the country from a small, centrally governed collection of states depending on excise and import taxes, to a powerful nation that fought two World Wars and became the dominant global powerhouse with vast revenue, much of which came from the federal income tax. Although this is true, the statement does not reflect the progressive negative nature of a tax based on income and the harm that this form of tax does to the country and its people. It has gradually reduced individual freedom and greatly expanded the bureaucratically controlled federal government.

As a concept, a tax on income was certainly not novel. It was well known in ancient Rome and no doubt in civilizations that came before.

Income tax in Britain was introduced by Prime Minister William Pitt the Younger in 1798 to pay for the upcoming Napoleonic Wars. Pitt hoped it would raise £10 million in the first year. The final total was apparently just over £6 million. Other European nations also brought in an income tax around the same time, so the U.S. was probably a century late in arriving at the table.

Interesting aside: Earlier, in 1707, Britain implemented the "window tax." Wise men of the time assumed that the number of windows in a building rated the wealth of the inhabitants. The base rate was set for up to 10 windows, with a graduating scale as the number of windows increased. Wise people can levy a tax on anything!

During the height of the Industrial Revolution and into the late 1800s, another revolution was gathering power against the monarchies and entrenched rulers of Western Europe—with good cause in many cases. The despots, especially in benighted countries like Russia, ruled with an iron fist and the agricultural countryside still lived in conditions reminiscent of the Dark Ages.

In 1848 the Communist League commissioned philosopher/journalists Frederick Engels and Karl Marx to write what became the Manifesto of the Communist Party. First published in London, it became the handbook of revolutionary thought sweeping through Europe.

I find it curious that the Communist League had to pay to have it written. With Communism/Socialism being such an emotional movement, could the League not find someone who would happily volunteer to write it for nothing?

Changing the face of Europe was more difficult than most socialists had imagined and many of the popular revolts were quickly and brutally put down. Tens of thousands of people perished or were forced into exile. There were a few successes. Serfs in Austria and Hungary were freed, and representative democracy was introduced in the Netherlands.

In the midst of this upheaval, Marx and Engels developed the Communist version of a "new world order" which, they promised, would bring about a better life for the masses. In fact, in the opinion of many, it brought enormous power and untold wealth to a few, and indescribable misery to millions. They had not replaced the "system" with a better model, they had just replaced the individuals at the top and nothing much changed for the masses.

I mentioned earlier that my father believed that the 16th Amendment in the United States (Income Tax) opened the door to the 18th Amendment—Prohibition.

At the turn of the 20th century, the Temperance movement was sweeping across the U.S. as the social and economic devastation caused by alcohol became evident. There was also another less apparent cause—the sources of drinking water were becoming cleaner.

Prior to that time, drinking water, especially in urban areas, was often contaminated and deadly. Beer was the everyday drink of children, who would graduate to gin and whiskey as they became older. It's often (correctly) stated that much of the Western world was in a constant state of inebriation for centuries—including the U.S. The fact that a good deal of the work and debate that resulted in the country we know today as the United States took place in taverns should tell us something.

As long as the country depended on alcohol taxes to pay the bills, prohibition was dead on arrival. The new nation would be bankrupt almost instantly.

In the City of Reading, with my father as a mid-level City official, I witnessed (or was told about) how America changed in the first quarter of the 20th century—all from a socialist viewpoint.

In short form, the country went from an agricultural backwater to an industrial powerhouse funded by a tax on income (while still maintaining the existing import tariffs and tax on booze, of course), into Prohibition and the opportunities for crime, the rise of the Mafia, the cooperation between the prohibitionists and the socialists (strange political bedfellows indeed) and the evolution of socialists becoming Democrats. During much of this transition, I was a dorky, dyslexic ORK who, like the ugly duckling, was shunned and then finally accepted and educated by my parents as a likely future leader for the cause.

In my mind, Reading was a microcosm of everything that was happening in the country. It's probable that my father was one of the folks going to Canada, loading up their vehicle with Canadian whiskey, and bringing it back to be sold at a very high profit in the Reading area. There were expenses, naturally. A number of palms had to be greased between Windsor, Ontario and Reading.

Although I have no real evidence, I honestly believe that the team he led as "city clerk" was the strong arm of the city administration, and the corruption within that body that was run primarily by the Jewish Mafia allegedly controlled by the Minker brothers. Abe and Alex Minker also owned a number of legitimate businesses in the Reading area (including the White House Market where I stocked shelves) but were known to be in charge of the booze, prostitution, and gambling outlets. Slot machines were a common sight in virtually all of the so-called private clubs as well as alcohol because of the state's blue laws that prohibited the sale of alcohol on Sunday. Punch boards and pin-ball machines with cash payouts, to draw the young were available at the convenience stores on most street corners within the city. Although I never questioned him (or even asked my mother) I believe that my father may have been involved in the corruption as an enforcer.

I recall, while in high school working as a groundskeeper at the Reading Municipal Stadium, (a patronage appointment provided to me by the political influence that my father projected even after he passed) noticing a rough-looking man staring at me as another was pointing me out to him. As he came closer, I realized that he had been a prize fighter. Back in those days they didn't stop fights when a boxer was merely hurt—they waited until he was near death. Fighters carried the evidence of their profession: Their ears were exploded, nose squatted, lips scarred, and over their eyes was mostly scar tissue.

"Your name Wanner?" he asked without introduction.

"Yes," I replied.

"Your father Al?" My father's name was Alvin, but everyone called him 'Al.'

"Yes," I said again.

"Well, I fought for your father," he said simply.

He introduced himself and gave his name that he also used during his ring career – "Red Delp". We ate our lunch together and I had a very satisfying experience listening to a person that had been a friend and business associate with my father. He never mentioned being an 'enforcer,' in the local Mafia organization although I assumed he had the size, and physical presence to operate in that type of role.

One thing he did say that has stayed with me: "The only person I ever feared fighting was your father."

Al Wanner, Superintendent of the Reading Asphalt Plant, town official in charge of clerical staff, strong-arm enforcer (possibly), rumrunner, basketball player, boxing trainer, reluctant husband and father, socialist, my father, was very much in favor of the 16th Amendment and advocated strongly for the 18th Amendment. He had reasons.

He'd had a harsh life. A major part of socialism is the contrived warfare between the rich and the poor—the bourgeoisie and the proletariat. He saw life from the point of view of the poor masses and compared it to the rich, gravely noting the disparity. So, it was natural at the time for him to consider socialism as a superior approach and he was, at least in the beginning, a true advocate. As time went on, he may have seen the negatives, but perhaps he was seduced by the power he achieved, and so continued believing that he was helping to develop a utopian society.

My parents, although they supported the 18th Amendment banning alcohol, said they never stopped drinking during prohibition. In fact, my mother said that prohibition fundamentally changed the American woman. Before prohibition, she reported, women didn't frequent bars, and if they did, they were 'floozies' or prostitutes. Women certainly drank, but they did it in private at home. As soon as the speakeasies and clandestine drinking spots came along, women started wearing short dresses, smoking, dancing the Charleston, and drinking—much as the men did.

Promoting the War

One of the prime tenets of Socialism is promoting the war between the classes: the proletariat are at war with the bourgeoisie (poor / rich). We now have wars between classes, racial identity, genders, have and have-nots, educated and uneducated, urban, and suburban and country dwellers. Stay tuned. New conflicts will break out when the socialists identify a need to advance their agenda.

Over time, my father told me often, he saw the extremes of Socialism/Communism in the Soviet Union. He also saw the effect of Fascism under Hitler and Mussolini and knew that Socialism (in its extreme form as Communism) could not succeed. That's why, I believe, that he and other Socialists switched first to a Fascist centered approach to government and finally to the Democratic Party, which they thought they could penetrate and influence. (The Democrats, in turn, were happy to add to their numbers, even if the new recruits were out in left field, so to speak.) The Socialists were not really changing their quest, just their name.

The income tax concept has become so ingrained in this country that all political parties now take it for granted and never question its effect. The general population seems to accept it as one of those inconvenient necessities, hold your nose, deal with it, and move on. It is a major industry that employs hundreds of thousands of people, both in government and the private sector.

When tasked with thinking about alternatives to an income tax, such as a 'consumption tax' or sales tax, people often respond, "a consumption tax is regressive and negatively impacts poor people the most." That may fly in the face of funding policy in states like Alaska, Florida, Nevada, South Dakota, Tennessee, Texas, Washington, and Wyoming which do not levy state income taxes. New Hampshire doesn't tax earned wages. With a few exceptions, the median tax rate on goods and services in Florida is 6%, probably not that onerous even for 'poor' people who would otherwise pay an income tax on earnings. And a consumption/sales tax has many other advantages that I'll discuss.

Our founding fathers conceived of the United States in an era that they understood. However, the world changed after that, and not all of their concepts withstood the test of time. The people who could affect change chose not to, either from conviction or ennui.

Therein lies the problem that provided a perfect field of windmills for an old reborn Don Quixote like me.

Marie and Dick at the Senior Prom.

Marie and Dick.

The Wanner Brothers.

The Wanner wedding party—1953

Dick Wanner— 12 years old.

"Mom"

Dick's mother, Ruth Miller, as a young woman in her twenties to thirties. Ruth didn't like photos of herself and throughout her life continually cut her image out of the pictures.

She missed this one.

MY FAMILY BACKGROUND

17 YEARS OF CONFUSION, TRAUMA, & POLITICS

By the time I was about 17 years old I'd accomplished a lot in my short life.

The most recent accomplishment—I had graduated from Reading High School at the bottom, or very near the bottom, of a class consisting of 678 students. That is somewhat of a guess and might be overly optimistic. Not an auspicious start you might conclude. But just graduating at all was, for me, a major triumph. And, at least, there were a few other diehards below me. Mostly guys I might add.

I had been run over by a car, (a new subject to be explained later) been an ORK (One Rotten Kid), arrested for break and entry and released (son of one of the city's leading socialists and all of that), had been abandoned by my parents and farmed out to relatives, taken back by my parents and thoroughly grounded in socialism by my father, crashed weddings looking for booze, and had started a 67-year relationship with my soulmate, Marie. Plus, a lot of other activities that I'll later chronicle on these pages.

Perhaps I should start at the beginning.

Other than the few dry crumbs of my own personal life that I will detail later, I don't really remember a great deal about my past.

According to the available records I was born Richard Alvin Wanner on September 15, 1933 in Reading, Pennsylvania to Alvin and Ruth Wanner (née Miller).

I believe that my father was a member of the Socialist Workers Party of America at the time. I'm not sure if my mother was ever a card-carrying member, or if she just went along with my father. The Socialist Party controlled the politics of Reading for a number of years, and the mayors and councilmen were all socialists. Al Wanner was certainly very popular in the town. On the day of his funeral at Miller's Funeral Home, the line to pay respects stretched for blocks.

Dad (I called him "Pop") and possibly my mother were ardent believers in socialism and saw nothing wrong in absenting themselves from the responsibilities of raising their own children. In fact, deep within the socialist concept is the notion that children should be born and then handed

My father, Al Wanner. had a "commanding presence," very athletic; could run like a deer and swim like a fish. About six feet tall, he played semi-pro basketball and was a center on his team. (Today he wouldn't even be tall enough to be a guard!)

Reading & Northern coal-fired, locomotive.

Anthracite coal, stored in the tender car behind the locomotive, was burned in the boiler to create steam to power the Pistons.

The locomotive would have to stop periodically to replenish the water and coal supply. If the water level got too low, the engine might explode. If the coal was all burned, the engine would simply stop making power.

An "engineer" controlled the locomotive, and a "fireman" shoveled a steady stream of coal to keep the boiler hot. Of course, there was lots of smoke and coal cinders.

A favorite activity for kids was waving at the engineer – who usually obliged by waving back.

Reading was a railroad hub, had two stations, and the primary maintenance facility for the company

over to a more professional organization to raise and "indoctrinate."

My father sometimes made vague references to such a parenting approach.

One memory of living "at home" with them might provide you with an idea of my mental state at the time. There's the "dead dog" memory for example: We were apparently at some function away from home and when we returned my sister, Lew, started screaming at the top of the cellar steps. There, below us on the cellar floor, was our family dog—dead as a stone. I can see it to this day.

My thought at the time was that my mother had killed the dog. She often complained about looking after it, didn't want it in the first place, and I knew we had it only because Lew had successfully pleaded for it.

My mother had already flushed our goldfish down the toilet when she became less than enthused about having to care for them, or perhaps Lew or I had not taken responsibility for their welfare. I actually thought they would be returned, good as new. Never happened. Both noted memories occurred when we lived in a rental house at 1411 Church Street.

After my kindergarten year we moved to 545 Robecon, about 3½ blocks away and around one corner. Much closer to the elementary school at 5th and Spring where I had my first meeting with Marie,

my future wife and the mother of our three kids.

Most of my time when supposedly living with my parents at 1411 Church Street, was actually spent with my grandmother, Mary Miller, Aunt Laura and Uncle Jack Teasdale, and their son, my first cousin also Jack. Or with my next-door neighbors, Arthur and Mrs. Barkle. (Not certain of the spelling of their surname.) It was an absolutely wonderful escape from the difficult living conditions presented to Lew and me, next door, and life with my parents.

Sitting on Mrs. Barkle's lap listening to the radio was a heavenly experience. I can still hear the 30-minute radio programs The Shadow, The Lone Ranger, Fibber Mcgee and Molly, and my favorite, Amos 'n' Andy. Yes, I know I'm probably out of bounds for mentioning that last program.

Reading was a city of rowhouses, many of the men employed by the Reading Railroad (of Monopoly fame) The locomotives used hard anthracite, a type of coal that apparently burned cleaner and hotter than softer bituminous coal. You would not have known the advantage with all of the coal dust that covered the area and probably entered our lungs.

My sister Lew and I had a strange relationship with our biological parents. My mother never nursed me (or maybe she did for a short time), which was the way most babies were fed in those days. Apparently, I was given to my Aunt Laura Teasdale, my mother's sister, who had also recently given birth to her son, Jack. In later years she reveled in telling me that she had Jack on one spigot and me on the other. She had been my "wet nurse."

Aunt Laura told me that it was not that my mother did not want to raise Lew or me, just that she was too busy and had other interests at the time. A great cover story but it lacked a certain amount of credibility.

So, although I "officially" lived at home (1411 Church Street), I was unofficially fed and raised during my first years by Aunt Laura and the Barkles, (1409 Church Street). Both Arthur and Mrs. Barkles. were wonderful to me. As I mentioned earlier, Reading was a railroad town and we lived about a block away from the yards where coal-burning locomotives belched coal dust and smoke 24/7. We would often be sick from the dense smog. I recall sleeping while Mrs. Barkle ran a vacuum cleaner in the room. Vacuum cleaners in those days were like machines that redistributed the dust from one point to another. The sun was shining in the window, and I was mesmerized by the sparkling dust particles in the light like thousands and thousands of fireflies. I remember the event so well.

Many years later I went back to Church Street trying to determine whether my memories were real. The second-floor bedroom of the Barkle house had a bay window in front which faced west. In my memory it had been morning, since I was just waking up, but it had to have been late afternoon or evening, and perhaps I had been having a nap.

During that same visit to Reading, I tracked down another childhood trauma.

Throughout my life I've had crazy, vivid dreams in color. I also had a recurring nightmare which often started off like other innocuous dreams. Then I would be floating through walls to the outdoors to where there was a brilliant, brilliant light. I would feel ecstatic as I floated toward the light—it was like being released from a dungeon. But the closer I got to the light the more my pleasure turned to pure agony, and I'd suddenly wake up in a panic. I can only speculate now regarding the reason for the panic. Possibly the fear of the unknown.

Certainly not the fear of Hell, as my parents were not Christians and rarely spoke of faith, or the existence of God during the times I was home with them.

At Sixth and Amity in Reading, at the end of Church Street, there is still (or was) a playground, with a sandbox and a bright streetlight. I can remember as a youngster going into the sandbox and

My sister, Lew, and I. Lew was in third grade and I was in first grade. Notice the ears? For many years, my nickname was "Dumbo" after the famous Walt Disney cartoon elephant, whose ears were so big, he could fly.

The photo was taken in our backyard at 545 Robeson Street in Reading, PA.

545 Robeson St., Reading PA.

My mother decided to put a small retail store in the living room, but Lew was against that. So it was decided to locate the store in the basement with access through an entrance to be dug on the lower level.

My father was very surprised that I had completed the work in a single day. "Good job," he said. I think it was the first time he had realized what I could accomplish.

To the right of the railing is the narrow alley where I had pushed my trike after being hit by a car when I was four years old.

It was from here that my father and grandfather exchanged curses one Memorial Day.

covering myself with sand. I believe that my mind was fixed on the idea that if I was covered with sand no one could see me, and I'd be safe. I could hide in the sandbox and never have to go back home again—although I'm not sure which home I was living in at the time.

For some 50 years I had this persistent nightmare/dream until I returned to Reading and investigated the old playground. There was the pavilion with the sandbox and the streetlight in the same position as the bright light in my dream. Perhaps, at the time, my parents were having one of their frequent bad days and I just wanted to escape. In any event it was a trauma, and the dream came and went for years until I revisited the playground. I've never had that specific nightmare since my return visit.

In first grade, during one of the interludes when I was living with my parents, I recall riding my tricycle on the sidewalk near the elementary school. It was winter and there was snow on the ground. Lew, my sister, was ahead of me on her bicycle. Trying to navigate a sharp turn I hurtled out into the street and was hit by a car. I don't remember being hit, but I recall waking up in the arms of a woman wearing a fur coat. This was unusual, I thought at the time, the long hairs were greasy and oily, and I didn't know what kind of fur it was, but I remember it clearly.

She asked me if I was OK, and I assured her I was. Convinced, she deposited me on the curb, got into her car, and drove off. I was confused, no doubt in a state of shock, and was not sure if she had hit me, or if someone else had hit me and she had stopped to see if I was all right. Lew later confirmed that it was the woman who had hit me.

I must have been running on adrenaline because I pushed the trike home despite a bent wheel, and through a very narrow alley on the side of our house. I don't remember how but I also got it down into the basement and stored it at its normal place. I was probably thinking that It would never be discovered and the bent wheel would suddenly and miraculously be repaired. Then slowly I crawled from the basement inched up the steps to the second floor (the adrenaline was probably wearing off at that point) and crawled into bed for the next several weeks.

My parents found me collapsed and called Dr. Dash, our family doctor, who checked me out and couldn't tell them what was wrong. I was six years old, in trouble, and I wasn't saying anything to anyone.

Lew, who of course had witnessed the accident, tattled me out on the doctor's second visit. From that point on she became the 'official squealer' in my mind, and I never let her forget it.

Dr. Dash was understanding but said there was nothing he could do—just bed rest. So, I continued resting for at least a couple of additional weeks, feeling feeble and despondent. I don't remember how I got to the bathroom. But I do recall that my weekday midday meals were brought in by neighbors because my parents were working, and the 'official squealer' was in school.

Looking back, it appears my malady was much like a severe case of juvenile clinical depression, perhaps brought on by the move, our unsettled family circumstances, and any number of other negative factors in my life. The accident may have been the trigger that broke the dam and released the swirling darkness. Or maybe I just had a concussion that took time to heal.

Less than a year later, after more months of benign parental neglect, my maternal grandmother insisted that my parents give up Lew and me permanently, which launched three-and-one-half years of great turmoil, love, uncertainty, and sexual abuse.

It was a large household: Lew and me, my great-aunt Laura Kissinger (not the "Aunt Laura" who had nursed me), and great-uncle Gus, and a wonderful couple, Lily and Earl Lavan, and their son, Bob.

Seven of us altogether. Lew and I slept in a semi-finished attic that lacked heating. Lilly did insist that the door to the attic remain open on cold nights. Summers— You sweated as did the entire world during the early 1940s.

Lily, many years ago, had been a 'doorstep baby,' dropped off unannounced and anonymously years ago on Kissinger's front step, probably by an unwed mother or someone who could not look after her. She then became Aunt Laura's unofficial 'daughter,' and my unofficial 'mother' for the time I lived at 905 Greg Avenue.

Lily was wonderful and Earl was great. They were my "parents." Bob was my "brother." But my Uncle Gus was a pedophile who abused me and, as I found out much later, my sister Lew also. Initially I believed that I was the only person that knew about Gus and his awful desires. Later, I became aware that within the family all was known through direct experience. They choose to keep Gus a secret. On one hand I loved everyone except Gus. I despised him for the unspeakable horrors he inflicted on me. I couldn't tell anyone; I was ashamed, abandoned, afraid, and a child. Who would have believed me?

In the middle of sixth grade my parents decided to reconcile and live together again. (I assume that they had been living apart, although I have no proof of what that entailed.)

1152 Church St., Reading PA.

This is where Marie Foreman grew up—around the corner from each other.

The Foremans believed that if they provided a place for the children to hang out, it would help them stay out of trouble.

So I spent many hours (along with kids from up and down the block) on the Foreman's front porch "staying out of trouble."

One Easter Sunday my parents decided to dress up and take a walk in Charles Evans Cemetery. We took photos of each other and, with grass and open spaces, it was very different from the concrete and drabness of our streets.

Immediately prior to our return to our parents, Lew guided me to the house where my mother was living in a room, or small apartment, for a visit. I stood gaping at this strange woman whom I did not know wondering what on earth she and my sister were talking about. We spent the night with her, the three of us all sleeping in the same bed, returning to Lily the next day.

I knew who my father was. He apparently visited my Great Aunt Laura to pay board for Lew and I. I do not remember a single time that I saw my mother other than the visit noted above.

So, this stranger was my mother, not Lily. Lew and I were going back to living on Robinson Street, in the house where I had spent so many weeks recuperating after my tricycle accident.

Once again, I wrapped my mind around the ever-changing circumstances of my life and moved on. In retrospect, starting from that time was the first and only real meaningful association with my parents. My father became my father for the first time. My mother became my mother for the first time.

But there was no joy in the minds of Great Aunt Laura, Lilly, Lew, or me regarding the return move. We all sobbed with the expectation that two misfit kids would be returning to a world that provided so many horrible and devastating memories. It was sad to move out of the house where I felt loved by Lily and the others. I was overjoyed and overwhelmingly relieved to finally be free of Uncle Gus.

It was a pleasant surprise that when Lew and I returned to our parents that we experienced a shock that life was actually somewhat pleasant and rewarding. Our mother and father seemed genuinely interested in us and interacted in ways that were not present in our prior life with them. Our fear and that of Lilly and our Great Aunt Laura did not come to pass. With perfect hindsight I realize now the effort it must have taken on their part to alter their understanding of parental responsibilities and take the necessary steps to help us grow into responsible adults. I have used this experience to alter my adult life to become a better man. Sometimes change might be hard but in the end very rewarding.

Shortly after we moved back with our parents, my mother precipitated an event which was to have life-changing consequences for me. We went to the branch library on Spring Street, she chose a book and asked me to read it aloud to her.

I could not. I was in sixth grade and could not read a beginner book.

She was astounded. "What are you doing? Tell me what you are doing to read?"

What I was trying to do was to look at each word individually, try to understand what it meant, and know how to spell it before moving on to the next word. It took a while to explain that concept to her.

She gave me a puzzled look and, in a certifiable stroke of genius said, "You don't have to be able to spell the word to read it." No teacher prior to this life changing event had taken the time to address my learning problem.

The revelation that I could actually read without needing the ability to spell the words changed my life. I really believe that from that moment on I was a different person. Something finally clicked into place in my brain. I began to read—books, essays, articles—pieces that no one in the past had ever expected the class dummy to read. Interestingly, even today half of the words I read I can't spell, but for some reason I can understand them.

This did not mean that my ability to write improved significantly. Writing has continued to be a difficult chore. As I rose in the business world, I found that I could dictate reports and memos and have someone else transcribe my words. "Creative" writing has always remained elusive.

So, although I could suddenly and miraculously read, I couldn't successfully write the exams and tests that evaluated my educational progress. I remained the "class dummy" for the remainder of my public school experience including high school.

*The Wanners: Back L-R: Jim, Steve, Mike;
Seated Marie and Dick.*

Granddaughter Sarah and Andrew

Mike & Jane with grandchildren Hudson & Chloe

Top L-R Kim, Mitch, Megan, Jim; Bottom L-R Jake & Janie

Janie, Jake, Megan, Kim, Jim & Mitch

Laurie, Charlie, Steve

Jane & Mike

Kate, Hudson, Brendan, Chloe

Dick & Charlie

Charlie, Zach, Kelli

MY FULLY DYSFUNCTIONAL FAMILY

Most of my family lived in the immediate Reading area and to say that we were dysfunctional was an understatement.

Even though he lived within a block of us, I saw my paternal grandfather for only a few seconds in my entire life. One Memorial Day when I was about 12 or 13, there were parades, bands, flags, and picnics everywhere.

I was on the front porch with my father, preparing to go to Charles Evans Cemetery and participate in the official Memorial Day events. An elderly man walked past. The man and my father started viciously and loudly cursing each other. I was stunned; absolutely stunned. The elderly man kept walking, hurling curses at my father; my father continued to curse him back until he was out of earshot. Sweating and breathing heavily my father turned to me and in an unnaturally calm voice said simply, "That was your grandfather."

I later found out that my grandfather, McClellan George Rossman, also known as McClellan Wanner and perhaps other names, was a cruel and violent drunk who beat my grandmother and my father's other brothers. No idea how he treated his daughters. At family gatherings and in my presence, however, he was always referred to as "George—that SOB."

According to the stories, my father had a paper route when he was a child, delivering newspapers door to door. One day he missed a customer and was docked some money. My grandfather, probably drunk at the time, was so angry he beat my father unconscious. According to my father, his mother (my grandmother) was "wonderful," but other than that, I don't remember anything else.

The Wanner sons, including my father, had disowned their father years ago. I believe there were 12 or 13 total children although not all of that total survived childhood. When George (the SOB) died, the girls in the family had to handle the funeral arrangements. The boys would have nothing to do with him, even after he was dead. Absolutely nothing.

I have often stated in conversation that my two grandfathers single handedly brought about the 10th Amendment to the US Constitution because they were

Marie and I walk down from the altar at our wedding.

both incurable drunks. While one was vicious, my maternal grandfather was, according to my mother, "The nicest drunk you could ever imagine. He was a happy, pleasant drunk." The problem was that he spent every penny on booze, so the family had nothing. My mother, when she was young, had to go to work in one of Reading's many factories to buy groceries for the family and I believe that she always resented that.

There were two routes she could use to get to her factory. One was a long walk around the streets; the short cut was across a busy railroad bridge. She had to time her bridge crossing carefully to avoid the many trains that left the Reading railroad yards every day.

She was, I know, resentful of her father's drinking and the effect it had on the family, even though he was a "nice drunk." Finances, or lack of finances, were always an issue since her father's wages went to support the corner tavern, and she was also expected to be a surrogate mother to her two sisters, Laura and Edith.

Of course, as we all know now, Prohibition caused a steep rise in crime, ushered in the Roaring 20's, and did little or nothing to curb drinking. In fact, it probably encouraged more drinking.

People have a love and fascination for "prohibited" things.

Another of my pre-eighteen accomplishments was getting religion—at least I joined a church. But it wasn't to open the door to heaven for my immortal soul; it was to further the socialist cause.

I was about 13 or 14 when my mother said one day, "You must join a church." I was quite taken aback.

"You and Pop never go to church," I replied heatedly. "Why do I have to go?"

"Well, you," looking at me like "don't argue you little shit, "will join a church."

"Which one?"

"Talk to your friends." And that was the end of the conversation.

Accomplishing that goal of furthering the Socialist cause required that one

have a "standing" in the community. In Reading, good standing would include membership in an acceptable church or religion. I also knew that my parents were actively grooming me to hold high the red flag of socialism after they were gone.

I checked with my buddies, and they recommended a church two blocks away at the intersection of Spring Street and Center Avenue.

"What church are you joining?" my mother asked a few days later.

"St. Margaret's," I announced.

She paused and looked me square

in the eye. "No. You will not join that church. It's Catholic. Choose another church." I suspect that my father was behind that decision.

It wasn't that she was against the Catholic Church; she was against all Christianity—an equal opportunity socialist. At that time Reading was predominantly Protestant and the church I joined had to be "acceptable," that is, Protestant. That way, she believed, I'd have a better chance to enter and become successful within the Reading political environment. I joined St. Thomas Reformed Church, although my attendance was rather sparse. I wasn't joining to be a good Christian, my membership was to further socialism, and at my age ping-pong was much more important.

My father didn't approve of my ping-pong habit, although I was a very strong player. He thought it was kind of wimpy. Didn't have any physical contact, therefore it was definitely not a sport for real men.

He had flirted with boxing in his youth, physically big and powerful, and later trained boxers in the Reading area. He did teach me to box, but since I had small hands and wrists, he knew that I would never make it in the ring. I doubt now that he ever fought professionally, as he also had smallish hands and thin wrists. Apparently, I did not fall far from my father's genetic tree.

I arrived home one evening after I was supposed to be in catechism class at the church. I just had more fun hanging out with the gang; possibly at the recreation center held at the 5th and Spring school gym. "What was the subject tonight," my mother asked nonchalantly.

"The resurrection," I responded brightly and with considerable gusto.

"That's good," she said a bit ominously. "I had a call from the pastor, and he doesn't remember you being in the class." I must have swallowed my lie with a big choking sound and was expecting to get the evil eye from Mom. Instead she actually understood my lack of enthusiasm for church and merely insisted that I maintain a better attendance record. That spurred me to improve my attendance and I did get confirmed as a church member, but it still didn't make me a very good Christian.

I remember asking the Pastor "How do we know Jesus was dead when they brought him down from the cross?"

Instead of answering the question, the cleric berated me severely for not having the faith necessary to be a good church member. He was quite unpleasant about the whole thing.

"OK," I thought. "I won't ask any more

questions. I'll do my own research." I've spent much of my young adult life investigating, reading, and trying to understand the religions of the world. I read the Koran and the Hindu holy book, Bhagavad Gita. I studied Buddhism and Daoism, and read all the sayings of Confucius. So, the minister's rebuke sent me on a lifelong spiritual quest. I don't have any definitive answers, but I certainly have a lot of information.

My other major accomplishment prior to turning 17 was Marie Elizabeth Foreman. When I say "my accomplishment" I can't take any credit for it. It was completely engineered by Marie. If I had had my way, it never would've happened.

She saved my life when I was sixteen years old. For reasons which neither of us have ever been able to explain, she invited me to a formal dance.

If there were ever two people who were poles apart, it was Marie and me.

Marie was attractive, a sparkling personality, smart although not a great student, cheerful, a class leader, and loved by everyone. She was compassionate, thoughtful, and never forgot a face or a name; easily the most popular girl in the school. She could have had multiple dates for the dance just by announcing she was available.

I was a morose and angry loner,

shunned by most, a one-time felon, the class dummy, and an all-round ORK who had no compassion and could hurt people without feeling any guilt. For me the idea of going to any social event with other people was unheard of. Unless, of course, if it was a wedding (to which I had not been invited) where free alcohol was being served to guests.

Of course, there was no official alcohol at the Y-Teen Formal, the group Marie had joined. I quickly discovered that a close dance with Marie was superior to any beer or shot of booze.

We had known each other since kindergarten, grown up together, and since Marie was friends with everyone, I was enamored. I thought of myself as inferior to her.

Over the 67 years we were together we talked about what brought us together. Maybe she was the 'good girl' who wanted/needed a 'bad boyfriend.' Or, a more likely reason, that my father had passed just prior to the dance and she felt sorry for me. At any rate, she asked, and I accepted.

Marie's parents and friends were not amused by our relationship. They begged her to end it. She persisted—for 67 years. My mother seemed to take it all in stride. Teachers and administrators at school begged Marie to drop me.

My mother, who was often abrupt and short-tempered, for some reason softened and helped me over the social obstacles, of which there were many.

My standard uniform then was jeans and a white T-shirt; the kind of outfit you'd wear while stealing gas and breaking into houses. A standard Fonzie uniform. "You'll need to get a suit," she informed me. "And a dress shirt and tie. And dress shoes."

"You'll have to buy her flowers—a corsage. And it better match her dress," my mother announced.

My response: "Flowers, she needs flowers"?

I asked Marie about the flowers. "On my wrist," she replied. "White."

My mother just laughed. She knew Marie would be wearing a strapless white dress.

The evening of the dance I drove over to pick up Marie in my stiff white shirt with the tie that threatened to strangle me; a suit with more pockets, buttons and folds than I could count; and new shoes that pinched my feet. The white orchid wrist corsage in the box was on the seat beside me. My hands were shaking and sweating; the butterflies were doing loops and hammerheads in my stomach. I wanted to punch somebody!

When beautiful Marie came into the living room in the strapless gown, I seriously thought about dying because

I knew I would never be happier than I was right then.

We went to the dance and for me, everything was a blur—a continuous kaleidoscope of sounds and colors and emotions. There are biblical stories of miraculous transformations happening in an instant. I felt that with Marie. I changed, not all in the magical biblical moment, but I can trace my change over the years from that one night. Marie was the 'singularity' from which The Big Bang emanated. The thought of ever hurting anyone physically or emotionally never entered my mind again. She changed my life so dramatically that I immediately evolved into a much different person than I had been.

Marie, the Y-Teen formal when we were 16. This is the first time we danced together to Nat King Cole's Too Young.

The Wanner Boys: Mike, Jim, and Steve.

Beach front vacation with grandchildren. Back L-R: Zach, Mitch, Jacob. Front L-R: Sarah, Marie, Dick, Megan. Kate is not in the photo.

56th Anniversary: 49-day cruise from Fort Lauderdale, FL, around Cape Horn, South America, to San Francisco, CA.

60th anniversary Alaska cruise. Back L-R: Jim, Steve. Second from Back L-R: Jacob, Kim, Zach, Laurie, Andrew. Third from Back L-R: Mitch, Marie, Kelli. Front L-R: Megan, Dick, Mike, Sarah. Kate is not in the photo.

FROM SOCIALIST TO DEMOCRAT

Another event took place about this time that was beyond my ability to understand: The leopard changed its spots. According to my father most of the members of the Socialist Workers Party of America changed their allegiance to the Democratic Party. In hindsight analysis, it made political sense for them to do so.

At that time World War II was just over, and the Allies had fought both against and with Communist and Fascist partners. With Fascist regimes in charge, Germany and Italy were certainly Socialist, as my father would attest. As our bitter enemy, we shunned their socialist political aspirations as unAmerican. The ethnic cleansing that took place, particularly in Germany, was abhorrent and horrific to most Americans.

The Communist USSR, once our ally, was becoming our worst nightmare as the east and west slid into the Cold War years. News stories of the stunning lack of success of socialism leaked out of the Soviet Union along with the excesses and purges orchestrated by Joseph Stalin and Lavrentiy Beria. There were famines and failed Five-Year Plans.

People began to realize that socialism did not offer a utopia; it had faults and many of those faults were extreme.

Also, Americans (at least in that era) did not like to be herded and told what to do, where to live, work, or what to believe. It's built into our pioneer DNA.

Seeing the writing on the wall— ordinary Americans were not going to embrace this brand of "socialism"— US socialists changed labels and became "Democrats." Except for the name, nothing else changed. They still embraced the "government dominance" rule of advancing their policies.

So, my parents were now avid Democrats, living and working in a Democrat-run city. My father was head of the Streets Department that included the asphalt plant, the base for workmen and materials to maintain Reading's street system. He was the foreman or supervisor of street maintenance, and was very hands on.

The street at the Seventh Street railway underpass (known to locals as "The Subway") flooded with each heavy rain—which was often. Part of my father's responsibility was to put up barricades to prevent people from

The switch from Socialist to Democrat made sense for the Socialist Workers Party of America.

driving through. On one occasion that I remember, he got there late and there was a car already stuck in the rising water. The driver was unable to escape. A phenomenal swimmer, my father dove into the rushing storm water and rescued the man.

If he couldn't locate workers during a storm, he would wake me up and I would assist in putting up the barricades. He gave me a lantern to swing in front of the barricades to alert drivers, inebriated or sober, before they reached the barriers, or me. I performed this job many, many times because my father always knew where to find at least one worker.

Eventually he was promoted to City Hall to become the head of clerical functions—much like a town clerk— issuing permits and recording documents. He reported directly to the council and mayor. It was a position of some substance in Reading and my father exercised a fair amount of influence. There were also rumors, unsubstantiated, that he was a leader of the 'muscle' that enforced certain decisions of the city and the shadowy criminal element that was always present. He certainly had experience from his boxing days and his work training prize fighters. His physical size and demeanor were intimidating, so it is possible that he doubled as an 'enforcer.'

He had a "commanding presence," very athletic; could run like a deer and swim like a fish. About six feet tall, he played semi-pro basketball and was a center on his team. (Today he wouldn't even be tall enough to be a guard!)

In those days—'20s and '30s—pro basketball was often played in a cage and the players were called "cagers." They could even use the walls of the cage to complete passes. One player shot all of the foul shots, and there was a center jump ball after every made basket.

They were "pros" because they were paid up to $25 a team for league or exhibition games around the Pennsylvania coal regions and Reading area. They took only five players on the road (more players meant less money per person and five could easily fit in a car), and no one ever fouled out.

As a boy, I was expected to be an athlete. Unfortunately, I was a sad disappointment to my father, although we both tried. Nor was I a good student. Two strikes against me.

Despite these failings, I knew that my parents had plans for my future.

Being able to 'compose'—to write— was critical to success in school. With the help from my mother, I had been able to break through the reading barrier and I certainly wasn't stupid in many areas. But I was always judged on my writing ability and my role as the 'class dummy' endured.

However, I did have the ability to absorb and process information, and to potentially lead people. Thus, my parents decided that my future lay in politics.

Socialist politics to be specific.

From that point on my father made it his job to teach the Reading, Pennsylvania form of politics to his son. Me. He would sit for hours talking in depth about the meaning of socialism and the various shades of the concept. Under Communism, the government and bureaucracy ruled every aspect of the country and the lives of the citizens. The people have no direct voice and while there may be elections, the Communist Party always wins by a huge margin.

He was more in favor of the fascist flavor of socialism that allowed limited free enterprise as long as the entrepreneurs followed the rules.

To my father, Fascism was 'socialism lite' (my words, not his), but politically viable. He taught me that Communism would always eventually fail. Being bureaucratic in nature, it didn't have the legs for long term economic viability, and the system would ultimately collapse in on itself. The then-current situation in the USSR orbit was confirming his analysis.

Fascism, he believed, had a more logical approach. Government would still be in control, but it would use the skills and assets of the people to enhance the country. Certain people, the ones who sucked-up to the officials and adhered closely to the government line, would prosper more than others.

He also acknowledged that creating a 'common enemy' was essential to the success of Fascism. Certain people or groups had to be demonized for the government to continue to control the masses. In Germany, the Jews were among those singled out. They, so went the propaganda, were responsible for the ills of the country since they were rich and propertied and refused to share their wealth with the common people (the proletariat, serfs, and poor). The solution was to purge them, and Hitler had a high level of support from Germans in his endeavors.

While unsettling, this was not necessarily wrong in my father's eyes. The expansion of socialism might require some collateral damage, but this was to be expected in the advancement of a progressive utopia.

There is parallel with current US political activism and the noted demonization application with both Communism and Fascism: The rich, white men, police, religious groups, gun owners, and all that not do not favor big

government policy, are met with scorn and in some cases criminal prosecution.

Our classes were not formal, but we discussed politics whenever we were alone or working together and, to give him his due, he was a great teacher. It was also a bonding experience that I enjoyed. We might be far apart in many areas, but at least we had politics in common.

He made little reference to the full US Constitution in our discussions, except for the passage of the 16th Amendment by Congress on July 2, 1909 and ratified by the required 75% majority of the US states on February 3, 1913. My father viewed this event as a seminal achievement and one that would eventually create a strong Fascist system within the United States.

The Congress shall have power to lay and collect taxes on incomes, from whatever source derived, without apportionment among the several States, and without regard to any census or enumeration.

The 16th Amendment brought the second plank of the Communist Manifesto into force in the United States:

A Heavy Progressive or Graduated Income Tax

To him it was a remarkable accomplishment that the US government (and its citizens) would willingly accept this steadfast socialist principle.

He also made the obvious link to the 18th Amendment, which we will talk much more about.

OPINION AND DOCUMENTED FACT

For those of you reading this in the 2030s and beyond, in my day (the late 1900s and early 2000s) we had two kinds of beliefs.

One was called "documented fact," among other names, for information that could be proven through public scrutiny, scientific investigation, and public polls. If you asked 100 randomly chosen Americans, carefully ensuring they fit a particular demographic, you could get a "picture" of that specific demographic at that particular moment of time answering that precise question.

There was a mathematical factor built in that could predict the maximum amount of variance one way or the other.

Question: How many heads do American men have?

Answer: One.

Most people will give the same answer. There may be a very few American men who are conjoined twins (in the past commonly termed Siamese Twins after Chang and Eng Bunker, 1811-1874—look it up!) and might in certain constrained circumstances be considered a two-headed man.

This would be called a "documented fact" and there are few who would argue with you. It is also a "commonly known fact" as there are not many people who know conjoined twins and are able to dispute it.

We also had beliefs, which we called "Opinions." and sometimes, "Faith," It was extremely difficult or impossible to prove, or disprove, an opinion, or faith. Opinions were offered freely as every opinion maker wanted as many people as possible to embrace his/ her opinion/ faith. Politicians, religious leaders, news/ journalists, celebrities, advocates, and activists are a few of this large group.

Question: How do we know that Jesus was real and died for our sins?

Answer: It says so in the Bible.

Question: Where did the Bible come from?

Answer: God wrote the Bible.

So, it appears that this is what my generation called a "self-fulfilling prophecy" or a "self-proving fact."

 "I am what I say I am because I said it was so. So there!"

As I've said before, Socialists want people to be divided and have common

enemies so they can blame their problems on someone else and rise up against the oppressors. It's the Magical Marxist Formula for revolution.

All of this might sound sarcastic, disparaging, in bad taste, simplistic, racist, misogynistic, non-inclusive, divisive, and personally offensive. That's why we have the First Amendment to the US Constitution. (Assuming we still have it.) But that's the way society is. Like or not.

Our job (actually now your job) is to respect everyone and allow them to have differing opinions (so long as those opinions don't involve physically or mentally injuring someone) and get on with your own life.

Sounds simple enough. Difficult to follow.

One more point to make.

In my day the mainstay of the US opinion delivery system was the "media" (broadcast, print, networks, and a lot of fragmented news/opinion outlets) that espoused liberal/Democrat, conservative/Republican (we only have these two legitimate political parties), along with Libertarians and others who fell somewhere left, right, or in the middle, along with blogs, podcasts, and other distribution channels.

By the numbers most of the mainline media fall directly into the liberal/Democrat (dare I say "socialist?")

camp. ABC, CBS, NBC, MSNBC, CNBC, CNN, New York Times, Boston Globe, Washington Post, Time, and so on. Leading the conservative/Republican charge is FOX News. What?? No one else? Well, there are a few small outlets, but nothing on the scale or reach of the mainliners.

With a bit of research, you can find out much more about this media war and how it has evolved over the past decade.

Now we get down to the nitty gritty about the media.

This is my personal opinion based on years of observation, investing, talking with media people, and reading about the business:

The media is a for profit business. It exists to sell ad space mixed in among news content and programming to provide a return to their shareholders. (Or else they operate on a subscription basis for the same goal.)

Next: And this is where the rubber meets the road (old 2020s expression. Means "Important.")

Most media have four "sweepstakes" weeks a year when third-party auditors measure the number of viewers/listeners/readers in a competitive market for each individual outlet over a multi-day period, ending up with cumulative reports on who had the highest rankings among various demographic groups (age, gender, household income, etc.) by time span and content.

Media outlets use this information to set their advertising rates for the next quarter. More audience + better audience = means more ad revenue.

While the third-party auditors are generally straight arrows, the networks and individual media go out of their way to goose the audience attention during sweeps. New programming is highlighted, specials and special news are promoted.

There are consultants who help with this process by selling the media particular promotions.

"Are our railway crossings safe for your children? Watch tonight's news at 11!" Behind the talking head is a film of a train crashing into a car at a level crossing somewhere. Nuts and bolts are flying everywhere and the crash sounds have been enhanced.

The film has been specially prepared by the sweeps consultants who did actually crash a car at a level crossing. They sell it to a station as 'exclusive within your market,' meaning that another station that overlaps within your market will not get that film or the come-on, but it will be offered to the next market over.

The stations pay large sums for this prepackaged sweeps material. They promote it as an audience attention getter, causing their local audience to question safety and to tune in for the answer.

Of course the answer is "Maybe" and the audience is no wiser when the segment finishes.

So, that is what I mean when I say that the media exists to sell ad space around the content.

A June 2022 poll by Gallup reports, "America's confidence in two facets of the news media—newspapers and television news—has fallen to all-time low points.

Just 16% of US adults now state that they have "a great deal" or "quite a lot" of confidence in newspapers and 11% in television news. Both ratings are down five percentage points since the prior year. Television news and newspapers rank nearly at the bottom of that list of institutions, with only Congress garnering less confidence from the public than TV news.

According to Gallup, 89% of Americans have little or no confidence in television news, so why do the networks have the big, overblown, prime time newscasts? If 86% of readers have little or no confidence in newspapers, why do newspapers continue to publish?

Since 1896 the motto of The New York Times has been "All the News That's Fit to Print." I'd amend that to "All the News that Fits Around the Ads."

And what about Congress? If some 90% of Americans do not have confidence in their elected

In the United States, unfortunately, much of the media portrays the country as being racist, intolerant, and racially divisive.

I do not believe this is true, at least to the extent that it is portrayed by the popular media. The effect is that some people who believe the media develop a negative attitude which drags down the culture.

I hasten to add that America is far from perfect, and changes are needed, but as a people, we are not so much the terrible ones depicted in the news.

– Dick Wanner.

representatives, why do they bother to even meet? Good question!

But back to The News.

News has functional time and space constraints.

TV news must fit into an allotted amount of time that has to include slots for paid ads. There are national ads where the revenue goes to the network; local ads where the revenue goes to the local station. The news editors have a choice: Run the story and make it as short as possible, or do not run the story. Lots of stories are produced that do not make the final cut and are never seen by viewers. It's a choice and the choosers are biased.

Newspapers are in a similar bind. If they are not running at least 60% advertising to 40% news they are losing money. News stories are written so that everything (who, what, why, when, where, and sometimes how) are in the first paragraph or two. If an editor chops the story off because of space limitations, at least the most important information is there.

Imagine chopping the bottom 50% of an ad off! Ads are revenue; news is just filler around the ads.

Thus today's "news" is constrained, limited, and biased.

Yet we are exhorted to tune in and find out what's happening in the world.

One TV ad drones: "More Americans get their news from ABC News than any other news source." God help us.

And don't think I'm being biased one way or another. Left, right, it doesn't matter. They are all guilty of the same offense. As readers/viewers we naturally base our opinions and decisions on what we read/see/hear on "The News."

And this is not new news. FOR EXAMPLE….

This is not "new" news. Jiggering the news has been going on for a long time…

How Moscow Bureaucrats Starved the Peasants in the Ukraine in the 1930s. (The Dick Wanner edition.)

As has often been reported in popular history, the grain crop in the Ukraine in 1932-33 failed and the Russian overlords took the crop to feed themselves, leaving the Ukrainian peasants to starve in the snow.

Well, sort of. What actually happened was rather more complicated and mundane.

One of the core policies of the Communist variety of socialism is "central planning." This is where centralized bureaucrats, who are mostly far removed (physically and philosophically) from those charged with executing their decisions, set quotas and production increases.

In this case the central planners (probably in Moscow) dictated the grain production increases they wanted, then tasked the local authorities to make it happen. The central planners, who could probably not correctly identify wheat from celery, had no idea what they were asking.

The local Party leaders knew full well that the required increase was impossible, and that the punishment for failure was possible death.

What to do? They did the obvious. They lied about the grain output, reporting production that was even beyond the outrageously unrealistic quotas.

The central authorities checked the numbers, left enough to feed the peasants (they thought), and took the rest of the grain to feed the urban population and to sell on the open market. Of course, because the numbers were so overstated, there was little left for the peasants, who starved to death by the tens of thousands.

It wasn't just grain. There were many incidents of factories making parts for machines and vehicles that, while actually producing little or nothing, sent glorious reports about overachieving their goals.

The vehicle assembly plant, using the nonexistent parts, sent on wonderful reports about the many tractors they had made, and the collective farms used the surplus of nonexistent tractors to help grow nonexistent bumper crops, which were sent to the cities to feed the starving inhabitants, who died.

The incredibly worrying part of this ridiculous scenario was that the bureaucrats who made the pronouncements knew about the whole ruse, but carried on as if it was genuine. Then they would increase the quota even more for next year. Everyone was deathly afraid of upsetting the few individuals at the top of the power pyramid.

One of the interesting facts of Chinese growth and production data is that every section not only meets their goals, it surpasses them every reporting period.

North Korea is even more predictable, while food production increases (at least on paper) more and more people are starving to death.

While, as my father would often point out, Communism as the core of socialism is doomed to failure because of the bureaucratic overload. So, here's the question: Is fascism, a socialist system that allows limited state sanctioned entrepreneurship and some local control, more likely to succeed?

There is a meme these days that states: "Socialism fails when it runs out of other people's money."

This probably explains a lot.

The Four Stages of Fascism

There are four broad stages to the lifespan of fascism.

1. The Expansion Stage

Fascists take political power as a particular identity-group so that they can use the power of the state to infuse private industries—owned or acquired by people in that identity-group—with public funds, seized properties, tax breaks, large exemptions, and other economic advantages that only political institutions can provide. This means that during the first years of fascist regimes, private industry sees a huge influx of wealth, which is little more than the concentration of broad public funds into preselected private hands.

That is what has happened in Russia over the past decade or so. So-called Russian "Oligarchs"—overnight multi-billionaires who suddenly own the national oil production facilities, mines, transportation, and production facilities. Friends of the government leaders display conspicuous wealth, move about the planet at will, curry favor with Russian leaders, and once in a while, fall out of favor with the rulers and are jailed; reduced to state criminals. (More of this is going on after the Russian invasion of Ukraine and the allied sanctions.)

2. The Honeymoon Stage

In this phase fascism looks good. The rich get richer, and the poor see a light at the end of the tunnel that could mean a better life for them. Previously scarce goods and services are available, and more people have more money to acquire them. The economy is booming or appears to be. The national leadership often begins to think of territorial and/or economic expansion—a move that is often supported by the majority who are now proud nationalists. But what appears to be happening is all-too-often an illusion. What is really happening is that the masses are starting to feel their power and, in both small and major ways, are challenging the order of things. Political leaders usually allow a certain amount of leeway for change, but they also see the likely collapse of their empire, loss of riches, loss of power, and loss of total control. Leaders may also create a "common enemy" as a rallying point to bring citizens together. In Nazi Germany it was the Jews, in more modern Myanmar it is the Rohingyas. "America" is often named as a common enemy in any number of cases. (At the moment America may be in the mid to late stages of this phase and entering Stage 3.)

3. The Repression Stage

At a tipping point, the aspirational demands of the masses outweigh the tolerance of the leadership. They institute a crackdown on dissent and "wrong thinking" that organically spreads to most sectors of the economy and may include purges of officials and leaders, censorship and forced closures of the media (except the "official" channels), civilian reprisals, arrests and secret incarceration, and closures of (formerly allowed) business that may suddenly be operating in a "traitorous" manner. At this point formerly available goods and services may become unavailable, certain mass freedoms and liberties may be curtailed, lowered production work hand in hand to promote shortages and inflation, emergency laws are enacted, and the leaders ensure that their stolen assets are hidden offshore and safe. Think Hong Kong in 2022.

4. The Chaos and Collapse Stage

Protest riots by citizens are put down ruthlessly, severe restrictions apply everywhere, travel and mobility are halted, and terror reigns. This is the end stage of the cycle and, phoenix-like, a "new" political system will rise from the debris. Whether the new system will also be fascist or not is difficult to determine. Based on history, some form of socialism/ fascism/communism is usually the ultimate replacement even though it may not have been the original goal.

If this seems depressing—it is. The reality is that the cycle can take several generations in the modern era, so it takes a while. Today's generation of young leaders do not have a personal understanding of the Cold War, Nazism, Fascism in Italy, and any history prior to 1980. They only know what they have read or been told. And that is suspect.

Richard A. Wanner

Marie hides a penny in her wedding slipper, an old German tradition that is supposed to bring good luck, on our wedding day, September 5, 1953.

DICK AND MARIE

With all the discussion regarding Socialism, taxes, etc. maybe it is time to switch subjects and discuss Dick Wanner, his history, and provide the reader with reasons why they should pay attention to his ramblings. Most important within the reader category, his family members that tend to limit his time behind the pulpit.

Currently the adult members of the Wanner clan do not necessarily view my memoir as a desirable task for their senior member. My evaluation of their attitude is simple: They reasoned the project was too close to Marie's passing and the need for me to relive past memories was not necessarily in my best interest. As it turned out, they were correct. In my defense, at age 88 when I started, I did not have the confidence that I would be able to complete the project in my remaining years. Another way to state my case, is that I was compelled to start and finish the task, regardless of any undesirable effect upon me.

Years ago, I saw a TV program featuring psychologists and other professionals interviewing and analyzing the personal backgrounds of known serial killers. Many of them had horrifying young lives. I could sympathize.

When you've been abandoned by your parents and have to live with a pedophile for three-and-a-half-years, when you can't read or write, and you're berated because school officials don't think you're studying—I don't know how in the hell I could have avoided behavioral issues. I'm not saying I would have killed people, but I don't know how I could have avoided being other than what I was. So, I do look back at myself as a teenager, and know that my evaluation of myself as an ORK (One Rotten Kid) is real and probably justified. Not much chance it could have been otherwise.

I agree with the "abuser-victim-abuser" cycle. My sister and I were abused—we were victims of abuse—and because of this we went on to abuse others. I don't mean that we went on to abuse others in the same manner. But Lew did have a difficult and sometimes chaotic adult life which I partly attribute to the wrongs she suffered as a child.

When Marie was in the last stages of PSP in Hospice care, and moved to a hospital type bed, she asked me to stay by her bedside during the night. I said that I would. Hours later, as Marie was in a deep sleep and I was achingly exhausted, I left for my own bed for a few hours. When I returned Marie was awake and looking at me accusingly.

I believe that I "abused" my family. Certainly not sexually as I had been, but in other words, ways: emotionally upset, not there when needed, placing my priorities over theirs, losing my temper over small things, ordering people about.

My emotionally absent childhood, moving from one home to another, suffering, the abuse, being the "class, dummy," and other traumas conditioned me to think that compassion and remorse were mere words without any connection to me.

After attending the Y-teen dance with Marie, I never again consciously thought of physically or emotionally hurting anyone, but the remnants of my reptilian brain did the work for me without me knowing.

The last time Marie and I danced together. She was very ill and it was a great effort.

"You left me," she struggled to say.

Those were her last words to me. I doubt that I will ever get over the event.

PROGRESSIVE SUPRANUCLEAR PALSY

I must describe Progressive Supra-Nuclear Palsy (PSP), in terms that a non-family reader might appreciate, especially those that have an association with family or friends that suffer from dementia. My family is well aware of PSP and the difficulty it presents to those afflicted with the condition. I'm on a quest to inform medical professionals and all individuals that have an interest in the subject, to be aware of PSP and that it mimics dementia. Individuals that appear to show signs of dementia, might actually have PSP.

From direct experience I'm aware of the lack of general knowledge of the condition within the medical community. Marie's cardiologist, and her family doctor were not aware of PSP and initially considered her condition as dementia. I had the same experience with many other medical professionals. Apparently, this lack of awareness is not uncommon.

Why is this important? With dementia there is noticeable memory loss. PSP does not have similar symptoms. Marie had almost total memory recall but had extreme difficulty in communication both verbal and through physical movement including facial expression. She was frustrated that individuals including her medical providers did not talk directly to her thinking that she would not remember any of the conversation.

MARIE

I knew Marie throughout most of my life. We started kindergarten together when I was six years old and lived with the Barkles, my wonderful next- door neighbors at 1409 Church Street in Reading. Marie lived at 1152 Church Street.

Between second and sixth grade I didn't see her, as I lived with my Great Aunt Laura, Uncle Gus Kissinger, Lilly and Earl Levan and their son Bob, attending a different elementary school.

Later we attended the same grade school through high school, and then 67 years of marriage. She is gone, but still exerts an astonishingly strong influence on my life. To say that she is constantly in my thoughts is an understatement.

Marie came into this world on November 8, 1933, the younger daughter of Edwin Harrison Foreman and Ada Marie Foreman. Ruth, a year or so older, was Marie's sister who married Eugene, aka "Yonk," Stief, one of my best friends from my ORK-y teenage years.

There was also a son, James Franklin Forman, who was 20 months younger than Marie.

Marie's father, Edwin "Dutch" Foreman was an alcoholic. To be charitable, he was a gentle drunk, who could drink more beer than anyone I have ever met. Because Edwin drank most of the money he made at his bakery job, Ada was forced to work there, too, just to keep the family in groceries—a common story in small town America at that time.

The five Foremans lived in a house co-owned and occupied by Ada's "Auntie," who raised the children, while Ada worked at the bakery. I believe Auntie's surname was Fischer.

That's not to say that Edwin (Marie's father) was a full-time slacker—he was a part-time slacker. Working the night shift, he would spend the first three or four hours working hard loading the bread trucks. Then his responsibilities changed; he drove one of the bakery owners all over Reading visiting the bars. He had keys to the clubs during and after Prohibition and, after dropping off his boss in the morning, he would arrive home thoroughly inebriated.

So that was Marie's young life: A happy, drunk father sleeping the day away, and a mother who worked all day and had friends and card games and a social life in the evenings. So, Auntie was her "mother" and "father." Marie mourned more when Auntie passed than she did her mother, Ada.

Everyone agreed that Marie was a very unusual person.

First, Marie was in my grade (that was not the unusual part), although I was relegated to the auto shop section of the Industrial Arts program during 11th and most of 12th grades. I was barred from the shop for fighting on the day my father died. I hurt the kid in the fight and still feel guilty about the event.

Marie was in the college prep stream with the ambition to become a nurse. And she lived right around the corner from me when I went back to live with my parents, so we saw each other often. We obviously didn't travel in the same social circles— she traveled with the elite because of her popularity. I traveled with great buddies who were primarily interested in raising holy hell and were rarely aware of any possible consequence. Two of the group became lifelong friends and remain alive to torment me with stories of my "bad old days:" Jerry Trupp and Eugene (Yonk) Stief. Yonk became my brother-in-law when he married Marie's sister, Ruth. I kidded them back, reminding them as the youngest member, they took me astray and forced me to engage in semi-criminal behavior.

Mom and me after Marie's accident that changed our lives. I was on leave after Boot Camp with the US Navy, and still had three years to go to fulfill my commitment.

Though fairly ordinary in appearance, Marie was by far the most popular girl in the school all the way from kindergarten to graduation from high school. She led the Majorette Corps which marched in the Macy's Thanksgiving Day Parade in New York City, was the Class Secretary in high school (the rules then permitted only boys to be president and vice president— secretary was the highest office a girl could hold), made good grades, and was a go-getter. During our years in school, there were actual popularity elections. Marie was voted most popular by a wide margin so noted the school paper. I spent my life chiding her that of the total senior class enrollment of 678, she received 677 votes. The only negative vote being her own.

In school she knew literally everyone by name, including all of the teachers, administrators, and especially the custodians, which will provide you with the scope of her very special and kind nature. There were 678 people in our graduating class—she actually knew all of them. She was also continually happy and positive. I recall a second-grade class photo where we were standing close to each other. There was Marie looking overjoyed and with the broadest smile ever. And there was Dick looking morose and joyless.

No wonder she was so popular!

Except for my immediate small gang of guys, I was not on any popularity list. We were into activities like siphoning gas from trucks to fuel our old cars, nearly getting caught at times—which made it all the more exciting. Long before the Wedding Crashers movie came out in 2005, we were in the same business.

While Owen Wilson and Vince Vaughn were looking for girls in the movie, we were looking for booze in real life. And we were very successful!

I also traveled with a different group of rabble rousers for a short time that really got me into serious difficulty with the law. Burglary (breaking and entering) was considered a felony offense and normally resulted in a trip to the county jail. My father, from his association with the city government, law enforcement, and the local mafia was able to extract me from the jaws of an early life of crime. He died within weeks after my case was heard by a juvenile judge and I was released back into civilized society. I never thanked him. Is that not a full and complete description of an ORK?

Marie's path and mine officially crossed in the spring of 1950 when she invited me out on our first date: a formal dance—the Y-Teen Formal. It may be difficult to believe, but I didn't know what a "formal" was. We could not have been more different. The bad boy and the good girl. Over the years we discussed it many, many times. "I had a feeling that you were way nicer than the way you acted," she told me. Not only was it my first date with Marie, but it was also my first date. Period. It was the first time I had ever danced with a woman. I had no idea how to act, and if it had not been for Marie taking the lead, I would no doubt have been a terrible embarrassment. It was also an emotional time for our family as my father had died just two months before.

THE NAVY

After that Marie and I could not be separated. We were like magnets, drawn together by invisible forces in a way that is hard to describe today. We spent long hours discussing our future together. Marie wanted to be a nurse, but nursing schools then did not accept married women. It was also the height of the Korean War, and the US was drafting eighteen-year-olds and sending them off to Asia. If we got married and immediately had a child, my draft might be deferred.

The other alternative was for me to enlist, rather than be drafted, and take advantage of volunteer benefits that might include not going to Korea.

Since I was seventeen years old (you had to be 18 to sign for yourself), my mother very quickly signed my enlistment papers and, three days after graduating and kissing Marie 'Goodbye,' I was in the Navy at boot camp—USNTC Bainbridge, at Port Deposit, MD on the steep bluffs overlooking the Susquehanna River just north of Washington, DC.

The next time I saw Marie was a month later at boot camp visitor's day. Half of our class got Saturday visitors; the rest of the visitors came on Sunday. I got Saturday, July 13, 1951. Bill Roth, an adult friend, and Kit, his wife and their three children Bob, Bill, and Ann, drove Marie to visitor day at Bainbridge. Bill actually acquired my old family car for the trip. Of course, there were plenty of other friends and girlfriends there, so we were never really alone, but Marie and I did spend as much time together as possible.

THE ACCIDENT

Not content with the Saturday visit, I also sneaked out on Sunday to spend time with other friends and parents who had come for their assigned day. Among them were Jerry Trupp, Ronnie White, and their parents—six of them. and it was obvious that they were distressed, and it had something to do with me. Just before they left Mr. Trupp took me aside.

"Dick, there was a terrible car accident on the way home yesterday," or words to that effect. "Marie is hurt and not expected to live."

In the Navy now... L-R: Dick Wanner, Ronnie White, Jerry Trupp.

The photo was taken the day after Marie's accident while I was at boot camp. Although I knew something was wrong, their fathers didn't tell me about the accident until the end of the visitors' day when they were leaving.

I was stunned and immediately wanted to go to her. But I could not get off base. "If the Navy wanted you to have a girlfriend, they would have issued you one!" kind of thinking.

Do I go over the wall? I asked myself. Jerry and the other friends there stopped me. I was frantic.

Even making an off-base phone call was an ordeal. Find a pay phone booth, stand in line, I'm begging the guys to let me jump ahead, and when you get to the phone there is a three-minute limit.

Get the operator, fumble in my money, Marie's parents answer. "What happened?" I scream.

On the way home from visiting me, in a town called Cochranville, a car ran a stop sign and smashed into the passenger side of Bill Roth's car—Kit Roth was in the passenger side front and Marie directly behind her. Marie was crushed; an event that would affect her adversely for the rest of her life. The ambulance took Kit and Marie to the closest hospital: Lancaster, PA Osteopathic.

Bill Roth, the Roth's twin sons, Bill and Bob, and their daughter Ann were also injured, but not as seriously as Kit and Marie who took the brunt of the impact.

I was desperate for news, constantly on the phone to the hospital or Marie's parents. In a couple of days, they said that she was expected to live. Thank God!

We had planned to marry in the future but had put it off so she could pursue her nursing training. The accident, and the possibility that Marie might die, moved up the schedule. I scraped together every nickel, collected any debts owed, begged for some liberty (I got half a day), and my mother offered to buy the diamond ring for me in my absence. A friend drove me to the hospital, and I saw Marie and Kit for the first time since visiting day during boot camp. They were in a converted recreation area, about 15 beds.

Kit, in the bed directly beside Marie, knew what was about to happen—but it was to be a surprise for Marie.

One of the resident doctors took me aside, saying all of the appropriate words. "Before you give her that ring, I want you to understand something. It's quite likely that Marie will be in a wheelchair for the rest of her life. And she will definitely not have any children."

That slowed me momentarily, but it did not stop me. I gave her the ring and she accepted. We were engaged. It was joyous. Then I went back to the Navy, haunted the pay phones, endured the drills and lectures and bad food, existing between the calls and hearing her voice.

By good luck, my boot camp ended on the same day, months later, that Marie was discharged from the hospital. I took all of my available leave, carried her from the hospital to the car in my arms, and carried her into her home in Reading where her parents had moved a bed into their living room. I became her nurse, fending off the many visitors, friends, teachers—we were invaded by the whole community because she was so popular. Me? I was just incidental, but I didn't mind playing my part.

"Can you get me to the football game?" Marie had been head majorette the prior year and they were expecting her. "Of course." I carried her to the car and carried her into the stadium. She weighed as much if not more than I did. In the stands they made a special place for her— fortunately for me, not all the way at the top.

As we were leaving the principal stopped us. Of course, he knew both of us—Marie was the golden girl; I was the troublemaker. They talked and talked and talked, and all the while I was holding Marie. At that time, I weighed about 145 and was in good shape, but still. I held on, not willing to give the principal the satisfaction of showing any weakness, fully understanding that I was not his favorite beau for Marie. I estimate that we were there for a good 15 minutes. I was shaking when I deposited Marie back in the car.

Life comes at you out of the blue and everything changes.

I took Marie back to Lancaster for a consultation with the hospital department head, who oversaw her care. "You stay here. You can't go back with her. I need to examine her very carefully." So, I waited and fretted and thumbed through old magazines.

Eventually he returned. "I know you and Marie have been intimate," he said. "And I'm going to tell you something right now. That resident who said she can't have children and would be in a wheelchair for life, well he was dead wrong."

It was great news, after months of bad news. We could get on with our lives— together.

But there were a few items to take care of first.

I owed Uncle Sam three years of my life and there was no way to get out of that. I reported back, attended two schools in Florida, underwent evaluation and testing, told them I wanted to be an air traffic controller. They told me I did not have the voice for it. Instead (typical Navy), they made me a photographer—a subject about which I knew absolutely nothing and had absolutely no interest.

That had never deterred the Navy before, nor did it now. I soon learned the fine art of taking photographs, developing the film, and making the prints. This was certainly not artistic photography, shooting models or flowers. I spent two years aboard a carrier (USS Wright- CVL49) photographing accident

Our first wedding anniversary in front of 545 Robeson St. on September 5, 1954. Marie is very pregnant with Steve who will be born on 9/24/1954, twenty-one days after after my discharge from the Navy.

Our wedding, September 5, 1953, Marie and I are flanked by our families and friends.

L-R:Eugene Stief (Yonk, Ruth's husband), Ruth Steif (Marie's sister), Edwin (Dutch) Foreman (Marie's father), Jim Foreman (Marie's brother), Ada Foreman (Marie's mother), Marie, Dick, Aunt Laura, Mike Shoppell, Ruth Wanner (Dick's mother), Laura (Lew)(Dick's sister), Grandmother Foreman, Douglas Rogers (Lew's husband), Mary Ann Teasdale, and Marie's Auntie Fisher.

On the table, left and right, are two 50-year anniversary candles. Marie and I would burn each one for an hour on our anniversary and play Too Young *by Nat King Cole. Today, after over 70 years, there is about an hour or two left on each one.*

scenes for investigations, some of them gruesome and unsettling. Then the carrier was reassigned to the Pacific and the Korean area where the war (or "armed conflict" to be technical) was starting to wind down.

I was transferred to the Quonset Point, Rhode Island Photo Lab where I was put in charge of the shooting crew.

The most memorable photo shoot of my Navy career involved recording the aftermath of a massive explosion and fire aboard the USS Bennington on May 26, 1954. It reinforced my decision not to stay in the Navy, even though I'd been offered incentives to re-up.

The short version is that, launching aircraft early in the morning, the ship's hydraulic catapult had malfunctioned, exploded and the massive cloud of oil caught fire. The human cost was 106 dead and 200+ injured. (The massive casualty list prompted the US Navy to change the catapults to non-flammable steam.)

I was called out to assist investigators photo-document the tragedy. Although I never saw body parts. Just body bags, cold and lifeless, lying on the hanger deck with dozens of news photographers swarming about them attempting to take their gruesome news photographs. That sealed my final decision to forget a career as a news photographer.

Other than that, Quonset Point was not a bad place to work. I played baseball in the league. And I also got the good news that I was eligible to be released early. I was good enough at my job that they wanted me to re-enlist. But I had photographed enough accident sites and in June 1954 was planning to happily walk away as a newly minted civilian.

But it wasn't without a few wrinkles.

Marie and I had been married on September 5, 1953, and, by the time of my discharge a year later, she was very pregnant with Steve.

The team was having a party to celebrate a successful season and I arrived late, grabbed a beer and was talking when someone hit a line drive toward me. I guess it was instinct, but I reached out to catch the ball, which hit the end of my left thumb and bent it backwards. Now the bone is sticking out, and I'm squirting blood.

The US Navy is odd. You cannot leave if there is something physically wrong with you that they might be able to fix.

So, I knew that a dislocated thumb with a compound fracture would cause some hesitation on their part. At the dispensary they cleaned it up and set the broken bone, but when I went to the Separation Center in the morning to get my papers I was greeted with, "I'm sorry son, you're gonna be transferred

*Marie and Dick
with Steve and Mike.*

Top: Steve is about one and, in the bottom photo Marie is pregnant with Mike. Our place was so small that "central heat" meant an electric heater in the middle of the room.

across Narragansett Bay to the Newport Hospital."

Newport, Rhode Island is a great place, the home of the Vanderbilts and Rockefellers, and other rich people we did not know. For Marie and me, it was one rented room, and I worked as the hospital mailman, using my good hand to deliver the letters and postcards.

Very near her delivery date, I drove Marie back to Reading and the apartment we had at my mother's house. I was alone back in the Newport Hospital and antsy.

Finally, I went to the captain. "Would you please let me outta here? My wife is pregnant and due in a few days. I need to be home so I can get a job and support my family." He took pity, I got my discharge, September 03, 1954. Marie and I started our civilian lives together.

WELCOME STEVE

My first need was to find a job because our son was coming soon. We welcomed our first son, Steve, to our tiny home on September 24, 1954. The car accident, a random and unexpected event, affected Marie for the rest of her days. She never completely recovered, although she appeared to live a full life, had three children, Mike (October 25, 1956) and Jim (April, 04,1966), went places and did things. She just never allowed her limitations, or the

restrictions that she endured, to slow her down. But she did bounce from one illness or problem to another for decades. She had had rheumatic fever as a child (it was fairly common back then) and that led to heart issues. Cysts in her breasts were an issue as she matured, and she had a series of operations including a double mastectomy. In the end, after a great deal of trauma and a stroke, she was diagnosed with PSP.

Looking back, my life has always seemed to be about the quest; and the more audacious the quest, the better I liked it.

This wasn't true about Marie—well, perhaps I flattered myself by believing that I was her quest—at least she initiated it, inviting me to that formal dance when we were 16.

Why then, would a teenager become a 'wedding crasher?' Surely there were easier ways to score drinks. But it was certainly spectacular and caused a great rush of adrenaline. Part of the quest had to be the risk. The risk of getting caught. The risk of failure. The risk of not being able to beat the system. Tell me it couldn't be done, and I was your guy.

I spent much of my energy, throughout my life, proving that it could be done and that I was the one to do it. During my 20 years with Sperry New Holland located in New Holland, PA, I took on increasing responsibility (without giving up any previous responsibility)—for what? To prove that I could. Perhaps. And there was always the incredible thrill of the chase, figuring out how to do it, executing the plan, proving that it could be done, savoring the personal accomplishment, and preparing to take on the next challenge.

Unlike Don Quixote, who ended up bested by the windmills he attacked, I was usually able to emerge victorious, if a bit tattered, at the end of the battle. Perhaps this spurred me on, and I lived from one adrenaline rush to the next, like a junkie whose high never lasts and is always looking for the next score.

While I was pursuing my next rush, Marie was raising four kids—of which I was the oldest. I often wasn't there. When I was physically there, I was more likely to be absent in mind, chasing a vague concept or an errant solution.

Steve, Mike, and Jim say that, as kids, they remember Marie and I always being there for their games and successes as they grew up. It was probably Marie who remembered the game time, venue, which son was playing, and so on. While they were on the floor or the field scoring baskets or runs, I was with them all the way. When they were on the bench or taking a break, I might be figuring out a particularly knotty problem of distributing harvesting equipment across North America. Or the world. Who knows?

What Marie thought of this I don't know. I don't believe I ever asked, I just took it all for granted. Perhaps she believed in the division of labor or responsibility. She played her role, and I played mine and together we eventually made a great team.

Though it appeared to me that she often played "second fiddle" to my quests, perhaps she considered that her "job" and approached it cheerfully and energetically. Certainly, she seldom complained and always went along with my wishes. I can truly say that she was my Sancho Panza, ever there with good advice (which I sometimes ignored), and tireless support.

Am I too hard on myself now? Is this how "normal" people actually live? Since my life has never really been normal, it's difficult for me to know.

COLLEGE AND ATLANTIC CITY

Even when I seemed to suddenly go off the deep end, Marie was able to make the transition and follow along.

For example…

One evening when I was 26 years old and we had two young sons, owned a very modest home, Marie was not working, and I had a basic low paying job with Parrish Pressed Steel as a time-and-motion study analyst. I said to her

The Wanner Family about 1968.

The Wanner Family in the stocks at Colonial Williamsburg. Mike and Jim, Dick and Marie. Steve took the photograph.

41st anniversary, 1994

The antique clock behind me, much prized by the Foreman family, has a story. Many years past, fumbling around in the dark, I accidentally knocked the clock to the floor. The vibration and resulting sound could be heard throughout the city or so I imagined. Fortunately for me, the glass front was not broken.

There was not a sound from Marie's parents sleeping upstairs.

Continued...

without a preamble: "I'd like to go to college."

That caused a long silence. "How can we afford it?"

Notice that she didn't say, "You're crazy. We have children to feed in case you hadn't noticed. You can't just go off to college. You have responsibilities! And what do you plan to study? How do you know you can even get into college?"

Marie knew me well enough to know that I already had a plan.

"Well," I responded. "I can still work part-time jobs. The tuition isn't that much. We can sell the house and move back into the apartment at my mother's. During the summers we can work at her hot dog stand on the Atlantic City Boardwalk."

It would be a grueling life for Marie, but I didn't let that hold me back.

My intent was to be an engineer.

I took the entrance exam. I doubt that I got any of the math questions correct, and the English, who knows? I probably scored a perfect zero, but I was admitted to Albright College in a general freshman class. Albright didn't even offer engineering, but it was my only portal into engineering at another school. We sold our house and moved back in with my mother.

By the end of the first semester, we were out of money. So much for my great plan. I said to Marie, "Either I have to quit or see if I can transfer to Kutztown," the state teachers' college.

"Do you want to teach?"

"Not really, but I think if I can just get a degree, it will help."

Obviously, I was desperate. I didn't consult Marie to see how desperate she was.

Plus, the tuition at Kutztown was initially $72 a semester, instead of the $400-$500 at Albright. We had to really scrimp even to get that money together, but we made it. I was on the Dean's List. The 'dumb kid' was on the Dean's List! Ha! Another windmill that lost the fight.

During the summers we lived in Atlantic City where Marie and I worked with my mother at her hot dog stand on the Boardwalk. It was leased from the building owner for $10,000 for the season (essentially the summer months) which is a lot of 20-cent dogs and 10-cent sodas. We also subleased part of our space to a palm reader.

My mother worked the morning shift along with me starting at 11:00 am. Marie and I covered the nights—Marie put in 70-hour weeks, and I called her a "part-timer." I worked a minimum of 100 hours a week, 14+ hour days.

Initially we hired college kids to work for us, until we realized that they were feeding their friends at our expense.

We decided to run the stand ourselves, staying open at night as long as there were people on the Boardwalk who might be hungry or thirsty.

Marie was a whirlwind. She worked 10 hours a day at the stand, looked after the boys, taking them to the beach, entertaining them, never complaining. We made it through each exhausting summer so I could finish college.

Our first year began on the biggest business day of the year (Easter Sunday) with the women wearing their finest new ensembles and the men in their best Sunday suits. We had a blasting nor'easter storm. A normal Easter would have represented $500 in sales. Our take for the day was one hotdog and two drinks. A great big 40 cents. If I remember correctly, we did have an adequate supply of adult beverages in the fridge back at the apartment. I finished those off by morning, although my mother and Marie did not take kindly to my extravagant behavior. Steve and Mike just thought I was really funny. Jim was on the horizon not yet able to evaluate my unusual behavior.

The college months were not that much better in terms of sleep. One of the jobs I had was the night shift delivering bread and baked goods over-the-road for Maier's Bakery—the same bakery where Marie's mother and father worked. (They helped me get the job.) My route took me to Souderton, PA where I would exchange my load for their products, taking them back to the bakery in Reading, arriving home at 1:30 or 2:00 a.m., grabbing some sleep and getting up for 8:00 a.m. classes. Kutztown even had classes on Saturday mornings.

Marie was my savior. I believe that I was her tormentor. I felt guilty and unable to do anything about it. We were into this and could not easily get out.

Stressed out, sleep deprived, mentally and physically exhausted, financially broke, I was difficult to live with. I even found myself difficult to put up with. I ranged from argumentative to sullen to uncommunicative. Somehow Marie put up with it all. Maybe for the boys. Maybe she saw how hard I drove myself and appreciated it and forgave my difficult ways. Maybe she looked back at her own parents and figured that, despite having to deal with me, she had it better than they did. At least I wasn't a drunk (normally).

Eventually I graduated with my degree in teaching. With honors! I taught for a year and disliked it intensely. I bounced from one job to another, although each bounce took me to more money and responsibility. Marie's parents, who were of the one-job-per-lifetime mentality, thought I was just irresponsible. Her father barely tolerated me, even when he was sober. All these moves led me to New

New Holland logo, 1895-2008

New Holland was a global agricultural machinery manufacturer. Founded in 1895 and located in New Holland, PA. Today it is a full line provider of agricultural equipment and is part of Case New Holland.

It was acquired by Sperry corporation in 1947, then by Ford motor company in 1986, and then by FiatAgri in 1991, all prior to the acquisition by Case.

Holland, where I was to spend over 20+ years of my life as the 'go-to' guy whom they called on when there was a problem or things needed improving.

Steve, Mike, and Jim did their share of "kid stuff," played a bunch of sports with a considerable amount of local acclaim, obtained reasonable grades in school (better than their Dad) and rarely got into trouble. So, we did well there. I can now say with conviction that the boys (now grown men) represent the one single accomplishment that together Marie and her hubby, achieved. All who know us give Marie 80% of the credit, relatives and friends 10%, and Dick stretching for the balance.

Marie and I were a team even though the balance of responsibility was a bit lopsided.

Those windmills never knew what hit them!

NAT IN A NUTSHELL:
THE ODDS ARE HEAVILY STACKED AGAINST SUCCESS

After a few thousand years of accumulated written history, you would think that we humans would have learned a few things. Apparently not.

For instance, we have not learned things like price controls do not work (suppliers simply stop providing the goods and services when they no longer make a profit); increased government intervention Usually increases, rather than decreases inflation (too much money in circulation leads to devaluation); and socialism does not work in a modern society (humans stubbornly refuse to play by the rules).

Politicians, however, are not dissuaded by past failures. They keep recycling the same old "solutions" hoping for a different outcome. We all know what that defines.

When the Founding Fathers of the United States of America wrote the Constitution and accompanying documents, they were certainly aware of history—European history at any rate—which had been primarily monarchical and feudal up to that point. Thus, they did not have any firm models on which to base a national financing solution.

Monarchs in old Europe simply grabbed whatever they needed from the nobility who, in turn, gobbled up the resources of the peasants they "owned," and the emerging middle class who were paid to manufacture and trade.

Our Founders put a tax on imports (tea, cloth, trade goods, etc.) and "local" beverage alcohol. All of these categories were considered "essentials" by many of the newly minted Americans who paid the tax to get what they wanted. Of course, there were uprisings, rebellions and riots, but the excise taxes continued on with only sporadic interruptions.

These measures were sufficient to keep the young nation mostly out of debt until the Civil War. President Lincoln flirted with an income tax, which was enacted and then repealed when the War was over. But the country's infrastructure was growing rapidly, it was taking on costly international responsibilities, and national financing was increasingly tight. The Founding Fathers would never have predicted it.

Finally, the 16th Amendment to the US Constitution was ratified on February 3, 1913, and established the right of Congress to impose a progressive federal

income tax. Most of the states, with notable exceptions, soon followed suit. During the past 109 years an enormous alphabet soup of additional taxes, fees, levies, and charges have been enacted and added. In some states there are taxes on the taxes. It's a mess.

The main problem with virtually any income tax, in this writer's opinion, is that it is "leaky."

People may self-report lower than actual incomes through all manner of dodges. There are thousands of pages of exceptions, carve outs, and deductions. There are barter deals among individuals and companies, delayed payments, offshore accounts, and outright fraud.

Want to know more? Pick up almost any publication or broadcast reporting financial news.

Last I checked, the whole income tax act, including the accompanying case law, totals some 176,000 pages. The IRS employs about 80,000 full-time people. They have a budget well over $11 billion and may soon receive another boost of

$80 billion over the next eight years from Congress. In 2020 the IRS collected close to $3.5 trillion from American taxpayers. They also refunded more than $740 billion for overpayments.

Then there is the time and dollar cost of individual and corporate income tax filing, which is immense, difficult

to measure, and wasted. (If it could be calculated at all!). The change could potentially result in additional profits that will be used for efficiency improvements, increased wages for their employees, and best of all, charitable contributions to the communities and nation.

There is no known way to eliminate the income tax leakiness and other poor results associated with a progressive tax on income. There are far too many holes to patch. The only alternative is to start over with a different strategy. If you were to calculate the efficiency rating

of maintaining, enforcing, and filing the income tax it would be reason enough to consider a new more effective, efficient, and simple system for all American citizens.

So, what's an alternative?

The Communist Party alternative would be for everyone to work for the state, and the state would allocate an allowance for each worker. Since no one would own anything and private enterprise forbidden, it would work only in theory. Stalin and Mao tried that in the USSR and China without lasting success. The USSR failed as a Communist state after 69 years and China has transitioned to become moderately "fascist," allowing a measure of entrepreneurship outside of state ownership. North Korea applies a brutal iron fist cult-of-family and, outside of the family, there are no exceptions. Its national survival is tenuous.

Both Cuba and Venezuela are trying out Communism, but except for the ruling cadre, those countries are leaking people who want basic things like toilet paper, pharmaceuticals, baby formula, and food. There are other countries trying out various levels of socialism, including Canada and the US, but there are problems.

Besides being a financially "leaky" concept, the income tax concept does not factor in "people," and people are notoriously varied and difficult to herd. If people put in effort they fully expect to be rewarded and to be able to use that reward for something they want— otherwise, why bother?

I believe that most people want upward mobility; to work hard and rise in the ranks. In medieval feudal times the descendants of serfs could look forward to being serfs forever. The internet generation has seen the bright lights and the go-getters want more of them. Socialism is not the answer. Communism offers little mobility; fascism offers limited mobility so long as one abides by the Party rules.

There is, I believe, a growing movement in the US to rebel against this divisiveness, which, whether actually instigated and promoted by socialists or not, certainly plays into their strategy.

Finger-pointing is a "national sport" in America and listing any person, organization or group as promoting less than diversity, inclusiveness and equity will bring down the wrath of the cancel-culture gods from one side or another.

And I have not even broached the ever-growing national debt, immigration, the impending bankruptcy of Social Security, the post office, Medicare, Medicaid, climate, alternate energy, international politics, and other programs, plus the burgeoning additional spending programs before Congress and state legislatures.

One attempt to change the method used to obtain the revenue needed to fund the United State's government and eliminate the income tax was the Fair Tax. I was directly involved with this consumption based tax proposal and gave occasional talks on the Fair Tax plan to smallish groups in my local area In Florida. I devoted most of my time to alter many of the plan's features so that it was less confusing and actually saleable to the country. I failed miserably. The plan without the revisions that I proposed to the plan's managing hierarchy had one single attribute - It was superior to the income tax.

There is a solution that is fair (at probably the same or less cost to the taxpayer), equitable, driven by choice, and requiring a sea change in current

Don Quixote on an Argentinian postage stamp. The reason for the curved cutout on the front of the Don's "helmet" is that is was an upside-down barber's basin. The curved indent fit under the customer's chin to catch the loose hairs and shaving soap from the customer's face.

The story is pivitol to the mental stability of the old Don who insisted it was a battle helmet.

American culture, sure to be opposed by every socialist leaning politician and supporter, and probably will not be seen for many years—if ever.

It would lessen the power of government, give taxpayers a modicum of freedom, be flexible enough to meet national contingencies, provide simplicity, need only existing technology, be equitable across the board, and provide a feature that directly addresses and corrects for deficit spending by our federal government.

THE NATIONAL ACQUISITION TAX (NAT)

NAT (in my thinking) is a sales tax on every transaction for goods and services conducted at every level within the United States that uses the current IRS income taxing methods. It would replace all federal income taxes, as well as some other taxes based on income levied at the federal level. There might be room for negotiation on items like gas taxes, and the like. But for sure, no more income tax.

It works like this:

You want to buy a house, a car, a loaf of bread, or music lessons. Each purchase would be taxed at the same predetermined rate, which might vary from year to year, depending on the financial needs of the nation.

Extremely simple collection, pay as you go, using existing technology, low overhead, and fair.

NAT Reward #1: Up close and personal. Specific freedom/flexibility to determine how much tax you pay.

That is a huge benefit. Let's say you can afford a $4 million house and the NAT tax rate is 10%—you would end up paying $400,000 additional in tax. Now here is where "NAT freedom" comes in. You might say, "I don't need, or can't afford the house and the combined $4.4 million total cost. So, I'm going to buy a $300,000 house and pay $30,000 in tax. With NAT you have the freedom to make choices and decisions on your own behalf that will directly affect the amount of tax you pay.

Imagine going to today's IRS and saying, "Look, I earned $100,000 this year, but I really wanted to earn half that amount so I wouldn't have to pay so much tax. Can I catch a break here?"

If you're frugal and save your money (buying the lower priced house) you could invest the savings and see a return that would not be taxed until you spend it. If you choose to spend it.

Of course, you could decide not to buy anything and would not pay any NAT. (Yes, that's also ridiculous!)

A member of our family went to the Super Bowl on the other side of the country. After air fare, hotel, meals and drink, and a seat at the game, he was out more than $4,500. With NAT based at 10% ($450) his total out of pocket cost would be $4,950.

I (the thrifty one!) decided to watch the game at home on TV. I purchased a six pack of Highlands Brewing Company's Gaelic Ale, and a bag of Cape Cod russet style potato chips (my favorite). As I only drank two of the ales, and ate only half of the chips, I was out of pocket about $8.80. Of which $.80 was the tax. Not only that, I had a perfect seat thanks to the camera on a wire. With NAT it's your choice of how much tax you want to pay.

NAT Reward #2: Millions of hours and billions of dollars saved by people all over the country.

If you currently file a simple income tax return through a tax preparer online or in an office, you'll save a few hours and a few dollars. If you are currently self- employed with expenses and investments, you will save upwards of hundreds of hours plus. the cost of paying a CPA., tax prep or accounting firm, or an in-house accountant. If you are an employer there will not be any FICA or other monthly remittances to the IRS. Record keeping becomes much more simplified   you have already paid the tax. Those file boxes of receipts and paperwork can be recycled.

At the moment, there are all kinds of ways to avoid paying federal income tax. Under the NAT concept everyone is responsible for collecting NAT on their sales. The buyer pays, regardless if they are a government entity, business, or a private citizen / visitor, legal or illegal — there is no way around it.

The real question is: What are you going to do with the money and time you save by not having to file income tax returns?

NAT Reward #3: The existing social safety net programs can be refunded and updated.

Millions of Americans rely on federal, state, and local social safety net programs such as Social Security, Medicare/Medicaid, VA benefits, and others.

These millions also live in fear that the programs will run out of money before their need ends (or they die). NAT offers the opportunity for a "reset" in many areas at all levels. Government assistance programs should be included for updating and funding. NAT also offers a good opportunity to clean up government earmarks and other forms of "pork."

NAT Reward #4: Existing technology can easily handle NAT transactions.

NAT collection is "at point of sale." Forty-five U.S. states currently have a state income tax. They will be required

A 1972 Cuban postage stamp celebrates the 425th anniversary of the birth of Miguel de Cervantes Saavedra with a rendering of the venerable Don looking kind of wild and scary.

to add NAT to each transaction, collect and process the federal tax and forward the tax amount to an authorized agency within the federal government on a daily basis, after retaining a reasonable processing fee.

States that currently have an income tax will need to decide if they will retain the tax on income, or obtain their revenue needs through an enhanced sales tax or other source.

In the forty-five states that already have a state sales tax, the collection technology is already in place. These states will charge both the federal and state sales tax at the appropriate percentage, listing them separately on the receipt for the customers convenience.

Some of the five states that do not charge a statewide sales tax, do have a county option sales tax and most individuals within these states travel and are aware of the state applied sales tax process. In summary most individuals are aware of the sales tax concept and the change to this form of revenue generation should not represent a major a retraining issue

NAT Reward #5: Simplicity

There is a refreshing simplicity to the NAT concept. You want. You buy. You pay. You move on. No receipts to store. No IRS/FICA payroll deduction—you get to keep what you earn (+ 15.3% for working individuals). No tax documents

to file or payments to make. (No refunds either from your money being held by the IRS.) No more IRS audits—or threat of audit. Think of the enormous number of workers that could be shed from the IRS payroll along with registered agents, CPAs, and other income tax suppliers.

NAT Reward #6: Everybody still gets their share of the revenue.

Revenue sharing, transfer payments, and other tax sharing programs among the feds, state, regional, county, and local agencies continue as before. The difference is that now there is one collection point, making everything simpler, more cost effective, and faster.

I don't pretend to have all of the answers—I only know some of the questions.

SOME NAT DOWNSIDES (YES, THERE WILL BE SOME.)

NAT Downside #1: Hundreds of thousands of people will lose their jobs.

That's bold!

The staff of the IRS will be directly affected but the transition to NAT should be less stressful than I originally thought.

People will still be needed to manage and administer NAT, but the numbers will be much smaller.

While painful for those affected, there is a time delay prior to the enactment of

NAT that will permit an orderly transfer from the income tax to a NAT-based revenue system. Specifically, there is a six-month minimum period between state ratification and the start of NAT.

In addition, the prior year income tax audits should be performed during NATs first year of operation. An ample amount of time that provides for a smooth transaction.

As of financial year 2022, the IRS had 79,070 full-time equivalent (FTE) positions to conduct its work, a decrease of 9.1 percent since FY 2013. (From the IRS website 2023.)

About 150,000 IRS and US Treasury workers belong to the National Treasury Employees Union and I am sure they will advocate for a soft landing for their members.

It may appear crass, but many industries and organizations have gone through similar circumstances over the years—there are not many wagon wheel makers or butter churn manufacturers around these days. When was the last time you required a telephone operator to connect to your family or best friend?

How soon we forget the culture and job needs of the past.

The financial industry (CPAs, lawyers, registered agents, and others) will certainly take a hit. However, businesses will always need financial professionals for many reasons other than filling in IRS forms. Financial support people will lose jobs, but again, an aggressive retraining program along with retirement buyouts can help to alleviate some of the pain.

NAT Downside #2: The "NO NAT" supporters will launch a well-funded campaign that will be divisive, sustained, and focused.

A significant portion of the country will be either (a) against NAT, (b) for NAT, and (c) the remainder will be undecided and on the fence. Both pro and con sides will work very hard to sway the "undecideds" to their way of thinking. The media, on both sides, will launch scorched earth campaigns. Think of the American Civil War fought with electrons and ink instead of muskets and bayonet charges.

Resistance will range from "but… but we've always done it this way," to the "It's too radical and will destroy the planet!" Acceptance arguments might include everything from "Freedom!" and "Simplicity!" to "It will save the country!" "NAT will save us millions!"

NAT Downside #3: The Law of (Unintended) Consequences

Remember Newton's Third Law: "For every action in nature there is an equal and opposite reaction. That is going to happen if/when NAT is introduced. Some of the reactions we already know (the IRS will be mostly eliminated and there will

"The gratification of wealth is not found in mere possession or in lavish expenditure, but in its wise application."

—Cervantes

The Law of Unintended Consequences

There were also unintended consequences that the people who framed the 16th amendment would never have thought. For example, the IRS knows everything about everybody. Who would've thought that data capture would be a major result of the 16th amendment. Of course, the IRS will contend that your tax returns are private. History has demonstrated occasions when the privacy issue was severely tested. My view: with a consumption type taxing system there is no data to be captured and retained so privacy is not an issue.

be lots of "former IRS employees" around for a while), but the real challenge is that we do not know in advance what some of the unintended consequences will be. These will have to be dealt with on the fly by the NAT leadership team.

NAT Downside #4: Inertia

It may take miles to bring a supertanker from full stop to full speed. It is the same with embedded legislation. Income tax has been the norm in America for over a century. People are used to it. It seems like an enormous. amount of work to change the status quo. People don't like to do so much work, nor see such dramatic changes in their lives.

If you count the upsides and downsides, you can probably come up with an equal number of "downs" compared to "ups." But it isn't the number that counts. It's the weight of the benefit that counts, and in my mind, the weight of benefits inherent in NAT certainly outdoes the weight of losses.

So, where do we go from here?

I don't have the answer, just a proposal that I believe will reverse the downward slide into a Fascist- or Communist-based future for my beloved country.

Maybe we need a knight. Maybe one from Camelot; one with experience in the never-ending quest for the Holy Grail. Or a Don Quixote; with experience in fighting tenaciously for challenging causes.

Or just an extraordinary ordinary person who believes in the concept and has the energy, resources, and support to take it to market.

SMALL GOVERNMENT SOCIALISM - WITH A MORAL CODE

There are currently 27 Amendments to the United States Constitution. The 27th Amendment, in simple terms, prevents members of Congress from granting themselves pay raises during the current session. Rather, any raises that are adopted must take effect during the next session of Congress. It was ratified in 1992. (Being somewhat of a cynic, I imagine that #27 kept many in Congress awake at night.)

NAT - NATIONAL ACQUISITION TAX

The "28th Amendment" is a catch phrase for any number of possible/proposed amendments from setting an age limit on presidential office to removal of the president because of ill health. In my case I'm using the nomenclature to describe the yet-to-be created National Acquisition Tax fomenting in a few minds including mine.

In addition to NAT, I included other changes in my memoir that I feel are necessary or at least desirable to modify (in some cases scrap and start over) and reverse the inevitable slide into a socialistic cauldron. I list them here to alert you, the reader, that the issues will be addressed in detail later within this section of the memoir.

NRS - NATIONAL RETIREMENT SUPPLEMENT

NAT, if implemented, essentially eliminates one of the basic foundations of our current Social Security system that evaluates an individual's income and uses the lifetime savings amount to provide retirement benefits. Consequently, I provided a better approach that will add funds to a person's private savings at retirement that is based on age at retirement, and the number of months the individual has lived within the United States and paid NAT type taxes.

NHS - NATIONAL HEALTH SYSTEM

I feel the nation's health care system is deeply flawed and does not meet the fundamental needs of its citizens. I also agree with Senator Bernie Sanders that a national health care system is essential for the country to move forward in the modern world. So, read on to find out what I propose as a cure that provides federal government funded health care to each and every citizen of this country. Yes, NHS will accomplish that goal

A postage stamp from the USSR celebrating the birth of Spanish novelist and author of Don Quixote Miguel de Cervantes Saavedra in 1547.

without a significant increase to the bureaucratic nonsense that exists today, or a major cost increase to the national government and private citizen's budgets.

IMMIGRATION CONTROL

I believe immigration control is a major divide within the United States. So, I propose a system that will permit immigrants to enter legally, be identified with documentation, and have a clear path to citizenship. If the plan is implemented, it will greatly reduce the tension that is now part of the current political dilemma, provide the labor pool that we so desperately need, and continue a trend that builds a strong diverse population for the country.

ABORTION

John and I had a few contentious moments during the preparation of my memoir but none greater than my request to include abortion as one of my suggestions to improve our country's ability to fight the slide to Socialism. He actually removed the topic on one occasion and did not anticipate my negative reaction to his removal. Two thoughts as encouragement for your continued reading: I agree with the recent ruling by the Supreme Court that rejected Roe v. Wade but I also feel the ruling was horrible for the country and increases the tension that exists today within our society.

MY PROPOSED FIVE CONSTITUTIONAL AND LEGISLATIVE CHANGES

NAT - NATIONAL ACQUISITION TAX

A National single rate tax will be applied to all levels of government, all levels of business, all organizations including those identified of a religious nature, and all individuals within the 50 States of these United States on the acquisition of all services and products including resale products.

The proposed tax will be named The National Acquisition Tax (NAT).

A 7-year time limit is applied after passage by the United States House of Representatives and Senate for ratification of the proposed Amendment by the required 75% of State Legislatures.

Upon ratification by the required State Legislatures NAT will become effective on either the first day of July or January provided that a minimum of 6 months is available between ratification by the states and either the July or January initiation date for NAT.

Upon ratification of NAT, the 16th Amendment to The United States Constitution (The Progressive Tax on

Income) is repealed effective on the same First of July or January date that NAT is activated.

The rate of tax will be expressed as a single whole percentage as established by Congress using the normal legislative process including Presidential approval and may vary by month during the first 6/12 months following activation.

The single rate of tax must be reviewed and potentially adjusted on each succeeding January first based on the Total United States Revenue as compared to the total United States Expenditures:

When the result of the comparison of revenue against expenditures as defined above results in a deficit the single rate tax will be increased by a higher whole percentage to bring the revenue to expenditure comparison into equal balance during the year following the rate adjustment. The adjustment will use a 6% rounding factor to calculate the next year's single tax rate. A result of a 1.4% adjustment will therefore require a full 2.0% actual increase for the following calendar year.

To avoid disruption to The United States economy a 10-year window may be utilized regarding the rate adjustment process. Starting with the first year after NAT is activated, the actual rate adjustment may use an increasing factor starting with 10% and increasing to 100% during the 10-year window.

By example, after three years of NAT activation the rate adjustment would by constitutional law require a 30% factor to establish the new tax rate for the following year. Only 30% of the prior year's deficit would be used to establish the following year rate.

When the result of the comparison of revenue against expenditures as defined above results in a surplus, then 50% of the surplus must be applied to reduce a possible National Debt. The remaining 50% will be applied to a reduction of the tax rate if the amount of remaining surplus will provide a rate adjustment of one whole percent.

It will be Prohibited to utilize NAT in any form to provide welfare type benefits to any business or individual. Welfare benefits must be applied separate from NAT as a result of the normal and constitutional established legislative process.

ADVANTAGES OF THE NATIONAL ACQUISITION TAX (NAT)

Advantages of using (NAT) as compared with the current Income based system:

1.Reduce the opportunity for a socialistic based political system to use

class warfare as a means to obtain a voting majority in national elections.

2.Broaden the participating base of tax paying entities and thereby reduce the actual single rate tax (NAT). Examples include all levels of government and business as well as current non-paying individuals (visitors to the US, criminal operations, as well as all current non-paying citizens and non-citizens).

3.Voting citizens would have a much clearer understanding of the relationship between campaign promises and the potential impact to their actual rate of tax (NAT).

4.All tax paying entities would have an immediate and precise understanding of the actual tax cost on all acquisitions.

5.All working citizens and legal non-citizens would immediately receive a 15.3% increase to their take home pay by the elimination of the Payroll Tax (FICA). This change will have a positive impact to the working poor and reduce the normal regressive nature attributed to consumption-based taxing systems.

6.(NAT) is inherently fair to all tax paying entities as they will be paying the same tax rate in any one year. The rich will be paying a much higher total tax based on the toys and services they acquire.

7.Our government would by necessity become fiscally responsible and reduce the reliance on the Federal Reserve to establish a fluctuating interest rate and thereby reduce the risk and unfavorable effect of inflation.

8.The federal government will experience a significant reduction in the cost of managing the revenue function (IRS). Tax paying Citizens will avoid the necessity and cost of record keeping necessary to support the current tax filing requirements.

The primary tax collection process will be the responsibility of the states and duplicate the current requirement for tax collection that is now active in 45 of the 50 states of the United States. The 5 states that currently do not tax acquisitions will be required to add the Federal tax process within their state jurisdictions.

All states will transfer the federal tax revenue to the United States Treasury on a daily basis after subtracting their processing cost. This cost will be established by the normal legislative process of the United States Federal Government.

The noted process should represent a relatively simple modification to the revenue process that is currently in place within the United States and make the transition to (NAT) a walk in the park.

(NRS)

NATIONAL RETIREMENT
SUPPLEMENT

While it is unlikely, or even impossible, for the described 28th amendment (NAT) to be ratified, in the unlikely event that it is ratified, then we must provide a new

version of Social Security as a result, since SS is based on the taxing of income.

The following suggestion is provided to take advantage of the possibility.

All non-incarcerated citizens of the United States will be eligible starting at the age determined by normal legislative process to receive periodic payments from the US Federal government based on the following requirements:

Payment amounts will be established by the normal legislative process with approval by the sitting President. Payment amounts will not be adjusted for the reason of disability and will not be discriminatory for any reason.

Eligibility for (NRS) benefits will be based on the number of months citizens resided in the USA and either paid (NAT) or had the tax paid for them by a parent or guardian. Months that a citizen lived outside the USA will not count toward their (NRS) benefit calculation. Months

of incarceration will also not count toward the benefit.

Upon reaching a specified age as determined by the normal legislative process, citizens and legal non-citizens currently receiving (NRS) will be granted an additional benefit that is added to their (NRS) fund to assist them regarding the usual increase in their health care cost as they reach elderly status. Either an (NRS) supplement or an adjustment through the (NHS), but not both.

Citizens receiving (NRS) may discontinue the benefit and the resulting non-benefit months added to their future monthly benefit payment when they resume active participation in (NRS)

Non-citizens living legally within the United States and paying taxes under (NAT) will be eligible based on the months they participated.

A transition plan must be established to close out the current Social Security Plan and move to (NRS) for all current SS recipients and those approaching retirement age.

(NHS)

NATIONAL HEALTHCARE SYSTEM

Being a committed anti-socialist it might come as a surprise that I agree with Senator Sanders from Vermont that healthcare is a right and should be either added to the list of Rights as specified within the First Amendment to the US Constitution or added as a new standalone amendment. However, I differ from Bernie in one very important way. The government's role should be limited to a funding function and the actual management of health care should be the responsibility of private and licensed insurers.

All citizens and legally identified non- citizens will be eligible for (NHS) that live full time within the borders of the United States. US Citizens that live in another country will be eligible for (NHS) type benefits with the payment of a monthly supplement.

The actual payment amounts will be established by normal legislative process.

The federally licensed insurance providers will be allowed to offer health care type contracts to those individuals eligible for the program. It is assumed that a wide variety of health insurance types will be offered thereby providing the best level of care to the majority of included individuals. Each individual will have the option to select the best possible coverage to meet their individual needs.

Minor children will have the policy type selected by the parent or guardian responsible for their care.

The payment provided by the federal government of the United States will be deposited in the account for the individual with the selected insurance provider.

The included individual may add to the coverage amount in order to secure additional services or benefits. Employers of included individuals may also contribute additional funds to the selected plan, again to provide improved services or benefits.

Upon their honorable discharge members of the military services of the United States will be eligible for a supplement to the plans' payment based on the number of months they actively participated in military service. Reservists and members of our National Guard will also receive a supplement but at a lower standard when compared to full time military service.

All included plan participants will receive a supplement when reaching a specified age. The age and supplement amount to be determined by the normal legislative process. Note the potential for tho notod increase will not duplicate the increase within the (NRS). It will be applied either as part of (NRS) or (NHS) but not both.

All communication between included plan participants will be direct with their insurance provider. The United States government will not be directly involved with this activity other than to validate that a payment has been made to the insurance provider selected by the plan participant.

It is assumed that the above noted (NHS) will eliminate the current need for the wide variety of health plans that are currently provided by the federal government including Medicare, Obamacare, and the Veterans Services. In addition, many private companies might decide to supplement (NHS) rather than continue with their current private plans.

IMMIGRATION

Immigration is currently a major topic within the United States, specifically illegal immigration. Estimates are that nearly 20 million individuals reside in the US without a recognized identification as established under US law. The following suggestion is provided as a solution to the illegal issue and includes a logical path to citizenship for deserving immigrants and their minor dependent children.

The suggestion does not cover legal immigration as it is assumed that the US should continue with a robust plan that provides a path to entry, The following represents the sequential steps necessary to implement the suggestion to resolve the illegal immigration issue. It does not require the building of a border wall to partially control illegal immigration. If necessary the border wall has merit only related to terrorists' entry into the country.

Step one - Require all immigrants without legal status to register with an assigned department of the US government during a defined time period.

Step two - After the defined time period, unregistered illegal immigrants whon identified by any legal method would be subject to deportation.

Step three - Illegal immigrants that register will be vetted to determine if they are qualified to remain legally within the United States. Those that fail the vetting process would be subject to deportation.

Step four - Illegal immigrants that pass the vetting process will be provided identification that permits them to remain in the US. These individuals would be eligible for (NHS) but excluded from (NRS) unless they successfully completed the requirements that grant citizenship to immigrants. Upon the granting of citizenship the individual would be eligible for (NRS) including the addition of the months from their entry into the US and the date of citizenship to determine the (NRS) monthly benefit.

Step five - Business entities and all private individuals that hire immigrants must request documentation indicating the status of the requesting prospect. They must also verify the documentation with the responsible federal department to determine the accuracy of the employment request.

Step six - Businesses and individuals that knowingly employ individuals that do not have proper identification would be subject to increasing fines based on the number and frequency of the violations.

ABORTION

Abortion is and has been one of the most divisive subjects that characterizes our current political system. To me it actually represented the primary topic that prevented the Republican party from gaining a majority advantage in the U.S. Senate during the 2022 midterm elections. The topic also prevented them from achieving a much larger majority in the U.S. House. So, why would I enter the fray and open myself up to attacks from both my friends from the left and right? For one simple reason: The issue must be resolved if we are to reverse the Socialist slide.

The U.S. Supreme Court was correct in their 2023 decision to vacate the Roe v. Wade decision previously passed in 1973. Why? Simple, the prior decision was not Constitutionally based. It was in effect a legislative type decision that should be reserved for the Congress and President. The U.S. Constitution does not address the issue and therefore the Court does not have a dog in the fight.

'But,' and a very big 'but,' what a mess the Court has made of the abortion issue. Now we have 50 states attempting to resolve the unresolvable issue. What is a woman to do now that she must accept a state judgment regarding a very private and personal matter? Move, travel, seek an illegal abortionist within her state, or the worst option: Attempt to perform the procedure herself. Wow, what a choice she is forced to make. I'm quite happy that being a man I have not had to confront those options.

My suggestion on the abortion issue: While abortion is not part of the Constitution, what is the problem with using Article V to amend the document? Assuming that we could obtain the positive vote from 290 Congresspersons, 67 Senators, and 75% of the States, we might just create a miracle that would accomplish in my mind, a less conflicted country.

What would be the result of such a daring act? Women, doctors, and the U.S. population will have a clear statement of Constitutional law that defines for us what is right and appropriate regarding the abortion question. It will also provide a less divisive atmosphere within the country. Isn't that a good thing?

PROPOSAL SUMMARY

Time might be necessary to address, debate, document, and bring to fruition the five proposals that I listed above. Time that I do not have. It is wishful thinking for me to even contemplate their entry into a national debate. So what? I would not be mindfully related to Don Quixote if I did not try.

Note, that I referred to myself as an anti-socialist within my proposals. I use the term as it relates specifically to two areas of the current socialist approach to governance. The first is that history has shown that all transitions into a socialist based government have resulted in a massive increase in the scope and cost of government and the corresponding loss of individual freedom to the citizens of that country. This increase of government is applicable regardless if the change results in a fascist or communist type of socialism. The second negative factor of current socialism to me is the loss of a moral code in their quest to obtain the unannounced but obvious goal; a permanent position of power and control of all government functions. As my father suggested to me, collateral damage is occasionally necessary to achieve their intended goal; total power. Socialism's tactics to achieve this goal have included methods that resulted in the deaths of

millions and the loss of liberties to the citizens of the affected country .A strong moral code is not a necessary or desirable attribute in their quest for power.

My approach to governance is quite different. I approve of the announced goal of socialism that seeks a more balanced division of the nation's wealth. All citizens of the country must feel that their life has been rewarded and that they benefit from the policies of their government. A key element of my five suggestions listed above is that they minimize government participation in the activity and enhance the average citizen's life. They also are intended to reduce the cost of government by eliminating the huge build up of the normal bureautic structure associated with socialist governments. And most important, that the actions of government operate under the concept that a moral code is the key driver in the development of government policies and processes.

I can imagine what you, the reader, is thinking. That I was hatched, not born, and live in some kind spirit world that has no basis in reality. Your thought is basically correct, but in my defense, the thought that the United States is destined to become a fascist country does not provide me with pleasant dreams. Quite the opposite. I've lived a rather long life, seen and been instructed to understand the nature of socialism and its tactics, and now realized that the United States is at the brink of a socialist (fascist) success story. So, I had no choice but to present my theories and solutions to prevent the socialist takeover of our government and consequently the world. I thank you for continuing your reading of my memoir and appreciate the effort it took to get this far into the book.

Speaking of taking time, the 27th Amendment was introduced in Congress in 1789 by James Madison and sent to the states for ratification. It was not until 1992 however, after public displeasure with repeated congressional pay increases, that the required three-quarters of the states ratified the measure. Unlike several other recent amendments, which contained a seven-year time limit for ratification by the states (see for example Amendments XX and XXI) Madison's proposed amendment contained no time limit for ratification. Maybe we should make that part of the NAT strategy.

THE NOSTRADAMUS FORECAST

A CHANGE OF WRITERS

My champion writer, John Prince, was not able to complete this memoir and I'm temporarily taking over his duties. Hopefully he will be back, full speed and I can resume my assignment to verbally record my story and let John do his thing – making sense of my gibberish.

I also prepared the epilogue (the very last section of the memoir), in an attempt to again cover inadequately for John in his absence and move the project forward at sluggish speed. Hopefully to complete the memoir before I join Marie in eternal bliss. At 89 "I don't have much longer to go". That was actually a quote from Marie's father Dutch Foreman, when she tried to purchase new underwear for him. The old stuff was the embarrassment of the family. He was a character.

Personally, I hope to add a few summers to the current number 89.

This section of the memoir was intended to be my Nostradamus forecast of the United States and World if we are not able to stop and reverse the slide to either a Fascist or Communist form of Socialism. Current world events do not provide me with much hope regarding the reversal issue. We are at the end, or near the point in the slide, that a reversal will not be possible. As I write this section of the memoir, education is being replaced with indoctrination and our future society will have difficulty finding any reference to our past—our glorious past. Yes, I'm nostalgic—proud of it!

You are probably thinking how can I be so certain of future events on this topic. I will tell you.

Since the adoption of a progressive tax on income, the United States has been on a roller coaster that starts at the top of a hill and proceeds down with occasional pauses to the bottom and a certain abyss that results with either a Stalin or Hitler type in charge. Or Putin to be more current with the reference. The individual does not matter.

Only the concept that the world is in the process of converting to one dominated by socialist thinking. No other place or country other than the United States will have the means or resources to pause the slide, let alone reverse it. Sorry, that will not happen.

Old enemies do not go away, they just revive old strategies in new guises.

As I write this, Putin's Russia has invaded Ukraine and the war is in its second year with no end in sight. China is a tentative supporter, perhaps dreaming of annexing wealthy Taiwan. Russia probably has its eye on other conquests including the Balkan countries and a glorious revival of the old Soviet Union.

– Dick Wanner

What are the pauses I referenced in the slide? A few executive branch administrations within our government were able to tweak our income tax code and provide other legislative changes and Executive Orders that did pause the slide. Unfortunately, these temporary actions were reversed and the slide continued at the next election as the new administration reapplied the downslide momentum.

It is fair for you to ask—why is the type of revenue generation so important to the start and continuation of the slide that I referenced above?

Great question.

Because it establishes a class struggle that pits rich versus poor. There are always more poor than rich so elections tend to favor the political party that presents itself as the poor man's champion.

The highly progressive income tax is the perfect vehicle that supports socialist goals. Of course, those rich that jump on the socialist wagon benefit by special tax features that minimize the impact that a progressive tax has on their income and investments. Consequently, we wind up with a tax code that requires thousands of conflicting pages to hide the game that is being played at our expense.

It is also important to understand that the rich / poor issue represents just one of the many class warfare tactics that are employed by the socialist movement. The previously mentioned (gender, race, sexual orientation, ethnic origin, occupation, and a host of other convenient battle ground issues) are all derived and based on the rich / poor separation.

The illusion that by Taxing the Rich through a highly progressive income-based tax would eventually result in a socialist dominant system within the country was fundamental to their strategy. Note the second of ten requirements in the Communist Plank (A progressive tax on income). Actually, my father, Al Wanner, praised the original thinking that Marx and Engels used to build their strategy. I believe it has succeeded far beyond their original expectations.

Personally, I believe few individuals have accomplished more in changing the world than these two creative social thinkers. That compares them to Jesus, Mohammed, and Buddha, a trio that created change probably beyond their imagination.

The United States is the last obstacle in the way of a major conversion to a world dominated by socialist thinking. No other place or country will have the means or resources to pause the slide, let alone reverse it. Sorry, that will not happen.

So, what will our descendants experience after we all go 'bye bye?' Not a place that I would want to live as I believe you will agree if the following forecasted events actually happen.

• The central government will absorb a very high percentage of the country's wealth. Citizens will by necessity have less but government programs will be available to provide a minimum of services but also to control the population and maintain their place as absolute rulers of all aspects of a person's life. Guns you might ask? Are you crazy? Only for government personnel including IRS agents.

• There will be countries and borders but they will all have a socialistic approach to government control of the population. One main tactic they will apply to maintain control of society is to initiate a periodic conflict environment. I mean wars. Generally small, non-nuclear, but with nationalistic enthusiasm to maintain purpose and support for those in charge. Best of all, a need to build weapons, and all the items needed to support the war effort. I will let you imagine who the individuals are that will be invested in the war industry.

• Nepotism will reign. Almost back to the reemergence of Kings and Queens.

• The Constitution will be scrapped, a relic of our past and not referenced ever again. Laws will be dictated by the central government and changeable to meet their immediate needs. Crimes against the government will have the maximum penalties, yes even over crimes that would receive harsh treatment in our current utopia. Forget appeals, unless you spring forth with hidden wealth or admit your guilt and adjust to conform and be a "good" citizen.

• Education, forget it. All, and I mean all instruction will be to perpetuate government control and provide a cowed group of citizens devoted to their leaders. Remember German citizens were virtually unanimous in their support of Hitler. Putin still has a major portion of Russia's population supporting him in the Ukraine war. A government in control of the so-called news has a clear advantage of what the people think and who they support.

A special explanation is necessary regarding the new world order that I project as it relates to the Islamic faith.

Currently many Muslim countries support the rush to Socialism as it represents the demise of faith-based societies, (other than their own), especially Western Civilization, which is or was primarily Christian. Israel is a noted exception but I include them in my imagined new world order explanation.

Socialism and Islam currently have a similar relationship as existed with

the Prohibitionists and the Socialist movement during the early 1900s. They have virtually nothing in common except their desire to bring an end to Capitalism, and its accompanying individual freedoms and the various faith-based religions of the world.

I suspect this unusual marriage will have a rather quick and very messy divorce. It will end abruptly when my imagined Socialist States attempt to push their agenda into the Muslim world, or the reverse when an energized aggressive form of Islam seeks world domination.

Unlike the convenient conflicts between Socialist States, that are primarily intended to build nationalistic pride and fill the pockets of the ruling elite, battles between Socialism and Islam will be bloody and potentially nuclear. Both cultures have demonstrated considerable disdain for human life. Examples abound. There is a difference though between the two: Socialism simply accepts the world with a Godless or atheistic attitude. Islam is the opposite, demanding a strong allegiance to their God without dissent. Therein, lies the possibility, even probability of future new world conflicts. A suggestion for you youngsters, plan and be prepared to take cover.

Prior to the issue between the future Socialist world conflict with Islam, is the more immediate question, as to what will

happen when the freedom loving section of our society finally recognizes that the end of small government thinking is dead and will be buried? Violent revolution is a clear possibility. The January 6th, 2021, event at and in the U.S. Capitol might provide you with some idea as to the possibility. My feeling is that it could be more akin to the four-year violent struggle in Russia starting in 1917 when Lenin and his Communist supporters removed the Kerensky government and the Czar and family from the power base of the country. It was not a good time to be alive in Russia regardless on which side your sympathies lay.

Another theoretical issue that I will venture a guess - if all that I projected as stated above actually happens, and the world re-enters a period quite similar to what historians refer to as the "Dark Ages" what will be its duration and how will it end? For simplicity I will call this imagined period the "Bleak Period" to differentiate it from the time starting with the fall of Rome (9/4/476) and the beginning of the Renaissance in the 14th century (the "Dark Ages").

Quite frankly, I don't have a clue, but I will present just one possibility to stimulate discussion regarding the subject. A catastrophic event will take place (major volcanic eruption—think Yellowstone), that will block the sun and virtually eliminate plant growth for a minimum of two years. (Happened in the

14th century). No sun, no food, people starve and the earth is back to something akin to a primitive form of existence living. I'm not certain the survivors will be the fortunate few.

Civilization will have a new beginning and the cycle will be repeated. Question: Do you think it might be wise to maintain a minimal amount of fossil fuel production to use for power generation? Greenhouses with artificial light from fossil fuel just might be a good investment in this future imagined tale of woe. Might help some to survive the "Bleak Period".

By this time you must concede that I'm not going to win any prize for comedic writing. The big issue for me is that John Prince is not by my side, adding dry wit and a bit of pizazz to the story.

So ends the happy saga on our future earth and its people.

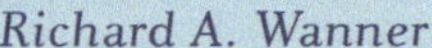

MARIE

A LOVING EULOGY BY DICK WANNER

Marie's passing was very difficult for me to accept. I realize counseling aids some or even most survivors of long marriages, but I must have been an exception. The therapist tried her very best but I eventually said to her that I was fine, moved on, and cried most nights when alone with my memories.

The family planned a private memorial for Marie that was to be held at son Jim's home. I understood that I would be expected to write or provide a few comments at the ceremony. Time passed and I agonized, delayed, and tried recording a few words on my phone. Nothing was acceptable. Certainly nothing that would adequately describe Marie and our long and memorable life together.

Finally, a glance at the calendar told me that time was running out and I forced myself to begin what was nearly an impossible task.

I wrote and continued for most of a month. The result turned out to be a eulogy that my sons and possibly their spouses did not want me to read at the ceremony. After some discussion they eventually succeeded in persuading me to omit portions of the document. I'm not certain today that my acceptance of their request was the correct path for me to take. Why? Simply put, It did not provide the closure and the need to move on with my life that I needed.

What follows is the original and complete eulogy. It was written when I did not feel up to the task or have the necessary mental equilibrium to proceed.

THE EULOGY

T hank you for your participation with me to honor Gum, Mom, and Marie. It means a lot to me that we can be together and share this special moment. For me her passing was in one way a joy in that it ended her suffering. But her absence from my life has been the single worst happening in an otherwise long and joyous life. That ever happy and radiant young kindergarten playmate planted a seed of true love deep into my heart, mind and soul.

I originally started writing this eulogy to Marie with the thought that I would enlist the aid of her family to read it tonight. Before the first word was transferred to the file I realized that your father and grandfather is the only person that could or should speak these truthful and penetrating words. Writing it proved to be one difficult if not impossible task. It forced me to remember every good and unfortunately bad event in the long journey that life provided us. Just thinking as to what I would say emptied my mind and heart as no other event during my 87 years. Being forced to confront the reality that I was an abusive husband to a true gift from god was the crushing result of my self-examination. I experienced every possible emotion but

Marie Elizabeth Wanner
November 08, 1933 -
September 17, 2020

On a beach vacation in North Carolina, hanging around out the pool with a drink. L – R: Steve, Mike, Dick, Jim in the pool.

Marie with granddaughter, Sarah Carney

most importantly the sorrow that now captures my mind.

Marie was remarkable, and I repeat, a true gift to us from a power beyond us. She demonstrated the one essential trait that proves that love is vastly more powerful than hate. My family must understand that Marie, their mother and grandmother, was filled with a boundless supply of love. While I, her husband and your father and grandfather had an equal filling of bitterness. No matter the reason for my attitude, there was a complete lack of compassion and most of all—remorse. My book of life includes countless times when I knew I had hurt friends and family, yet it never caused me a moment of pain or caused me to seek forgiveness.

My mind clung to the flawed logic that having received ill-treatment that somehow, I was permitted and blameless to transfer similar pain to others. To me I was a victim and those others were the villains. I could not understand that eventually the victim becomes the villain and who was to become my victim – none other than Marie and eventually our family. The very people that deserved my love and understanding. Anger is manageable but not to those that feel it can be justified by placing blame on their imagined villains.

There is a cycle in the villain, victim, and eventual conversion to villain process. Marie broke that cycle for me but it took years of patient and loving understanding. Her method was simple— to continue with a long and eventually effective combination of love and tender care. She never told me to stop doing something that I was doing or to do anything that would bring about a change in my attitude. She accepted my faults but reflected displeasure in the most respectful manner. I knew when she was displeased and eventually, after a long and painful struggle on her part I began to transform my life.

The sad part of my journey is that the answer was so simple and obvious.

My imagined villains were the victims themselves in a past that guaranteed the continuation of the process. I have recognized finally that my anger could only destroy me, not the people that caused the affliction. My greatest regret is that Marie is not with me to reap the benefit of my conversion and participate in the joy that comes with my living without bitterness.

MOTHER'S DAY

In writing today (Mother's Day), and listening and reading all of the email messages from you, I realize that Marie's greatest blessing was bestowed upon you—her family. That our three sons, six grandchildren, and soon to be three great grandchildren will all reap a special harvest of the love that Gum radiated. To those of you that joined the Wanner family through marriage I believe that you are also blessed by the positive effect that Marie had on your mate. So today remember that when that mate of yours plants a big hug and kiss on you—that Marie had a subtle hand in the transferred emotion.

In many ways Marie also affected the lives of her friends including those with whom she had minimal contact. The list of individuals that have phoned and spoken to me on behalf of Marie, made me realize the length of her loving arms. I was unaware of many of these associations and only realize now that she had a need to extend her love beyond the family. I long for her presence, her calm beauty and always will.

PERFECTION

I doubt the eternal question regarding the presence or absence of God will be answered in any human's lifetime. But with Marie the question was answered and she did believe that Jesus was divine, God does exist, and heaven is where the righteous will reside. If her version is correct then I have no doubt that Marie is at the highest standing within God's holy presence. Also I know that if heaven exists and that it represents perfection, then in some way she will find a hidden side entrance for me. It will take all of her silent but powerful persuasive ability so that I can join her in paradise. I'm also certain her family realizes that Marie and her husband must be united in body and mind if heaven is to be a perfect ending.

If the alternative to God and heaven is the true reality and at death we will enter an eternal everlasting sleep without dreams then I will happily accept that possibility. Understanding why is simple; Marie and I together experienced a true heaven on Earth. She was my savior, my love, and the source of all that was good in my life. My only unfilled wish is that I should have told her that I love her one more time.

The Wanner Boys: Mike, Jim, and Steve.

Beach front vacation with grandchildren. Back L-R: Zach, Mitch, Jacob. Front L-R: Sarah, Marie, Dick, Megan. Kate is not in the photo.

Mike with all of his futile attempts could not overcome my clear and perfect passes to Steve. The situation carries a lifetime of family humor. Steve was two years older, a foot taller, could run like a deer, and had hands like a gorilla. It would have taken a Tom Brady type quarterback to thread the needle and complete any pass to the frustrated Michael.

Over the past nine years I have received numerous complements in regard to the care that I provided Marie. Please understand that it was given with love but also remember that it was deserved. She saved my life and provided me with three sons that supported my theory that you must wait to determine the value of a grandfather by a close observation of the son's children – my grandchildren.

The jury is back and the verdict has been delivered. It was Marie not Dick that deserves the credit in raising – Steve, Mike, and Jim. My contribution was limited to washing faces during their nightly bath, telling bedtime stories, and developing their ping pong skills. I could also throw a perfect pass but only to Steve.

NOT SO PERFECT

There is a bit more to the story. It involves a requirement from Marie's Hospice nurse that she be moved to a hospital type bed. Steve is aware of the event and the devastating result that the move had on his mother. He assigned himself to her bedside the first night of the move. I had the second and last night that she used the hospital bed. Nothing has affected my current life as much as the events of that single night. I promised her that I would stay by her side. A promise that I did not keep. I could not

sleep and exhaustedly took a short nap in our usual bed. Waking, I went to her and she repeated "You Lied!" Using all her strength she actually used her left hand and feebly struck my chest, one for each cry indicating her displeasure at my lie. No physical strike has ever penetrated my soul so deeply.

Marie passed away a few days later. She never spoke or touched me again. Try with all my might I cannot get that moment out of my mind. Never will!

Quick decisions on the Florida move and other actions were an attempt to overcome my sorrow resulting from that single event. The changes have not helped and I have no confidence that a future change will produce any better result. I have come to one conclusion: God and heaven must exist and hopefully Marie will still need and accept me as much as I need her. I must tell her that I'm sorry for the lie and will devote myself to the task of restoring her faith in me.

65TH ANNIVERSARY

*Marie was in her 6th or 7th year dealing
with the ravages of PSP. I do not know
when the condition first started, but it had
advanced to the point that she required
constant attention that very quickly led to
Hospice Care. This note, while short, does
reflect some of the very good events in our
life together that needed to be shared with
her first, and now with you.*

Sixty Five, a special accomplishment
that is not achieved by many married
couples. But we are special and the
actual number is considerably greater
when including the years we spent
together in school and the time from our
engagement to the memorable September
day that you became my wife. It rained,
wow did it rain. All the friends and
relatives at the wedding and later at the
reception declared that the angels were
crying to celebrate our wedding. I do not
know if that was true but regardless we
accepted our fate and looked forward
to a life together with joy and a firm
determination to make it work.

Through the years we had numerous
milestones including the birth of our
wonderful sons and grandchildren. A
far cry from the doctor's dire prediction
that children were out and you
would probably require a perpetual
wheelchair as a result of the accident you
experienced after your visit while I was
in the navy boot camp.

One of many false announcements
from doctors that marked our life
together.

I stated accurately many times that
it was you that provided the firm moral
code and direction for Steve, Mike, and
Jim. A direction that is evident today
when I marvel at the men they have
become. For me I can only point to
their ping pong ability as evidence of
my participation in their life. Oh - how
I enjoyed the times we battled on the
table in the basement while you were
slaving in the kitchen preparing meals
for your four hungry gladiators. The
division of labor was not fair to you and
I apologize for my failure to assist you
in the household chores and all other
duties that you accepted without a single
complaint. Knowing that I will need
to answer for my dereliction of marital
duties is not an event to which I look
forward.

Throughout the many years that we
have been together, it has been my good
fortune that you have always been by
my side. Not only as my wife and the
mother of our three guys, but especially
as my very best friend. A friend that
healed my hurts and provided comfort

"It's a surprise party!!"

*40th anniversary surprise
party at Keowee Key Marina
hosted by the children and
grandchildren, September 11,
1993.*

The anniversary candles will have their 71st one-hour burning starting at 4:30 p.m. September 5, 2023. They were originally intended to have a fifty year life span. Note the box wine. Marie's favorite.

when it was most needed. Ignoring your own problems and the many illnesses that you endured, it was always your self-imposed duty to look to me and my immediate concerns. Looking back, I now realize that the very best thing that ever happened to me was you asking that I take you to the Y-teen formal when we were just sixteen and juniors at Reading High School. I remember that night as if it was yesterday. Beautiful does not adequately describe my reaction when I first saw you standing in the living room of your parents' home. I still think of bare shoulders, a radiant smile, and a look of anticipation as the best possible moment of my life.

Twilight time is now upon us. To many, including some family members, it might seem that it represents a burden without any reward. Nothing is further from the truth. Having you by my side represents all that is good and precious in my life. Each minute that I can hold your hand while we sit during the day, or hear your gentle breathing at night is a wondrous moment for me. Nothing this good can last forever but I look forward to many rewarding moments that we can share. Do not hesitate asking for my help on any and all chores. I owe you big time for the years of support and love that you provided to me, your appreciative husband.

Sixty-five sounds like a very big bunch of time. Actually, I don't understand where all the time went. I blinked and it was past. But I will state without any doubt that it was spent with you and a sense of wonder at the love we shared. How I wish we could do it all over again. Let us hope and pray that heaven is real, the future is boundless and we will be together in paradise.

I loved you in the past, I love you now, and I will love you forever.

EPILOGUE

BY DICK WANNER

John Prince is a first-class writer. He accepted my challenge to create a memoir for me that linked three entirely different concepts into a plausible narrative. That was the primary reason why I sought a professional writer to assist me. He spent many hours listening to my tale, researching some of my theories and putting it all in a form that I hope was understandable to the reader.

Attempting to link child abuse, Marie and her immensely strong influence on my life, and the political effect of Socialism on the American culture was a major challenge.

John was also able to tell a related story regarding my parents' abandonment of my sister Lew and me, and their later decision to become true parents in every sense of that word. Without my mother's (Ruth) attempt to understand my failure at school and the recognition of how it could be overcome was a special turning point in my life. She also was a very loving and positive influence for Steve, Mike, and Jim. Even though my father's (Al Wanner) concept of the proper approach to government was, and is, 180 degrees opposite to my current approach regarding the same subject, he was in truth the most effective teacher in my life. I owe him everything for my understanding of socialism and its history. Possibly we will meet again, and I can convert him to a small government, personal responsibility form of society. I would relish the opportunity. John was able to tell this part of my life effectively and I appreciate his dedication to record this part of my story.

I have added the following discussion covering the three reasons why I needed to write my memoir. If nothing else, they might also help the reader to understand me and my peculiar nature.

REASON 1

To describe what I consider the essential Constitutional and law revisions necessary to reverse the continuing slide of the United States into a Socialist economic system. The result could be either Communist or Fascist.

Since neither one would represent a positive change for the vast majority of the country's population, I suggest that the slide must be reversed. The five areas of change that I proposed within the body of this memoir represents what I consider to be the essential changes that together will bring about the necessary reversal.

I do not think of them as separate or independent from one another. To me they are the primary targets of the current Socialist attacks against the framework of the United States society and must be viewed as a combined area for a counterattack.

My father (Alvin) viewed the enactment of the 16th Amendment to the US Constitution to be the essential start of the conversion process that would guarantee that America would adopt a central power-based Socialist system. If he was alive today, he would be ecstatic at the progress that has been made toward this conversion. He would be most unhappy at his only son's desire to reverse the slide and return the US to a freedom- based economic system with greatly reduced central government power.

I view NAT (National Acquisition Tax), NRS (National Revenue Supplement), NHS (National Health System), immigration, and abortion as key elements in a reversal process. Readers might focus on other obvious areas for attention to enhance the reversal. I will applaud their enthusiasm for the cause and suggest they include the additions within their book. My inclusive changes I admit might only be a start.

The "Welfare System" might be a good place for an energetic freedom-loving thinker to start his or her book project. Frankly, I would start that subject with the elimination of all federal input into the welfare system and let the states control the process.

I did not discuss nor highlight Democrat/Republican issues within the book. To me, their current approach to national politics will only result in a guaranteed Socialist takeover of power within the United States. While there have been executive administrations of our federal government that created a pause to the slide toward socialism, none have demonstrated a resolve to reverse the process and deprive Frederick Engels, Karl Marx, and Alvin Jacob Wanner their posthumous victory. To the extent that I might provide a future charismatic and driven anti-socialist leader the tools to reverse the process, I will be forever proud.

Again, my five areas of change do not emphasize either Democratic or Republican talking points. If they did, the reversal I suggest would be doomed.

Instead, I tried to combine the best of both political philosophies into a plan that just might succeed, at least in my very active and Don Quixote-type imagination. If viewed from a benefit perspective, I suggest that the working poor of the country would benefit most from my proposals, which is hardly a Republican power base.

During my surprisingly long life, I have researched many of the world's most emblematic religious and philosophic leaders. Together they have provided me with the vision to propose the changes to our current Constitution and applied laws. The list includes Jesus, Buddha, Tao, and the current Dalai Lama. This group provided me with a direction that emphasized a moral framework to the proposals.

Confucius was the primary source of my desire to create a government that serves the needs of its citizens, not the reverse where the government has absolute control over the citizenry. Finally, Parmenides, a 5th century B.C. Greek philosopher who provided me with the understanding and need for a variable single tax rate within (NAT). I concluded the need to adjust the rate was necessary to control government extravagance and provide the voting citizen with direct input into a functioning government.

REASON 2

Marie, was my savior, friend, love, strength, and mother to our three sons. Her influence on me cannot be overestimated. If I contributed anything to our family and friends it was only because of Marie guiding me by using

the gentlest persuasion. In our 67-year marriage I do not recall one time that she told me to stop an action or start one. Instead, she proved that love is a more powerful force than hate.

I remember that a relative in the Wanner clan developed a chart that followed the family tree back to Pre-Revolutionary War days. The chart did mention the names of the female wives but provided no insight as to their history, just the men. It seemed from the chart, and I assume from most charts indicating family trees, that women did not provide an important link to our past.

I will not just admit but recognize that in my immediate family, it was Marie, not Dick that was the strength and moral foundation to me and Steve, Mike, and Jim.

Therefore, within the pages of my book I tried to inform the reader that it was vital that Marie be remembered. It is my hope that in an equal number of years into the future that equates back to the Wanner family tree, that a copy of this book survives to tell the story of Marie, if nothing more than to have some future Wanner, male or female, express the thought that "Wow, that Marie must have

been some woman". She was and, in my mind, still and always will be 'some very special kind of woman'.

REASON 3

I was recently at a friend's home engaged in a lively game of low stakes poker.

During the evening the conversation drifted to anger and the fact that two of my friends and poker participants had attended an anger management seminar. I casually mentioned that it might have changed my life if I had a similar positive experience.

Unfortunately for Marie and family that never happened. Instead, my young adult life was consumed by a sometimes-uncontrollable anger that did affect my family, especially Marie. While at work and in public with friends I was generally accepted as a reasonably controlled person.

They never knew, and would have been surprised, had they known that Dick would lose his cool with the least provocation.

Marie kept her cool, loved me regardless, and over time changed my life.

I would ask myself, why was I not able to control this hidden impulse to explode? It would drain me to my core and leave me exhausted, unable to function for a spell. Only through Marie's love did I eventually manage to escape this dual life existence.

But, the 'Why" question persisted.

Eventually I arrived at a possible answer.

VICTIMS OF ABUSE HAVE A STRONG TENDENCY TO BECOME ABUSERS THEMSELVES.

I have no statistics to prove or reject this self-identified pronouncement. I arrived at the conclusion only on the basis of reading a few articles covering mental health issues. Regardless, I do believe that abuse of a child is possibly the number one reason that starts or continues a cycle of abuse long after the abuser is dead and buried, or fried into disappearing smoke.

I often wondered if Marie had suggested that I seek professional assistance to identify the cause of my anger issue would this have reduced or even eliminated the problem. I will never know because she is no longer by my side. September 17, 2020, has become the number one worst day of my life. I deliberately plan activities on the date's anniversary so I can somehow endure the pain.

If asked, I would suggest that all people experiencing some form of abuse from a family member or friend, have the abusing or abused individual seek professional counseling. From experience it is necessary!

PEDOPHILIA

If you, the reader of this memoir, endured its content, and advanced to this position in your reading, then you might continue just a bit further and discover why the memoir actually exists. It was probably near Marie's death anniversary that I was watching one of the ubiquitous news programs with the normal talking head spewing forth news between advertisements that a short statement was read something to this effect:

San Francisco authorities are considering a revision to existing law that will decriminalize pedophilia…

Anger management aside I knew then and I know now that my inertia regarding the memoir was not acceptable. Being just one abused individual out of many was not an excuse to sit ideal while Socialist attitudes are hell bent on destroying this once great freedom loving and generally moral country. I immediately set forth on a quest to find a professionally gifted writer that would help me tell my story. Enter John Prince

in my life. John has endured illness that would stop lesser men and continued the effort. My gratitude to him has no limits.

PLEASE CONTINUE WITH ME FOR ONE ADDITIONAL EPISODE IN MY LIFE…

I was a child living with Great Aunt Laura, Uncle Gus, Lilly and Earl. We were at the kitchen table having what I remember as dinner.

The group in addition to me was my great aunt and uncle, Laura and Gus, and Lilly, my temporary but devoted mother.

Earl was probably at work and their son Bob had been drafted and serving his national commitment to the WWII effort. Sister Lew was either at school or enjoying life with her many friends.

I must have been whimpering with tears running down my cheeks. Lilly asked with her customary smile "What was my problem?"

All I could respond was "I hurt."

Her smile immediately vanished. There was complete silence for what I remember as eternity. My Great Aunt Laura must have been laser focused on her husband. I have no idea of his reaction.

After eternity ended Lilly rose from the table, came to me, gathered me in her arms and took me to the living room. We sat on the sofa and now there were two whimpering souls. I felt her tears drip on my face and realized that we now shared a common experience. One with a pain that never—never ends.

Please do not attempt to tell me that pedophilia is not a heinous crime and that a political system that lacks a moral code deserves to exist.